T0386692

MUSTANG II
& PINTO
1970 to 1980

MARC CRANSWICK
FOREWORD BY **JOHN H DAVIS**

4-Cylinder Engine Short Block High-Performance Manual – New Updated & Revised Edition (Hammill)
Camshafts – How to Choose & Time Them For Maximum Power (Hammill)
Competition Car Datalogging Manual, The (Templeman)
Cylinder Heads, How to Build, Modify & Power Tune – Updated & Revised Edition (Burgess & Gollan)
Distributor-type Ignition Systems, How to Build & Power Tune – New 3rd Edition (Hammill)
Ford SOHC 'Pinto' & Sierra Cosworth DOHC Engines, How to Power Tune – Updated & Enlarged Edition (Hammill)
Ford V8, How to Power Tune Small Block Engines (Hammill)
Harley-Davidson Evolution Engines, How to Build & Power Tune (Hammill)
Holley Carburetors, How to Build & Power Tune – Revised & Updated Edition (Hammill)
MG Midget & Austin-Healey Sprite, How to Power Tune – Enlarged & updated 4th Edition (Stapleton)
MGB 4-cylinder Engine, How to Power Tune (Burgess)
MGB V8 Power, How to Give Your – Third Colour Edition (Williams)
MGB, MGC & MGB V8, How to Improve – New 2nd Edition (Williams)
Mini Engines, How to Power Tune On a Small Budget – Colour Edition (Hammill)
Motorcycle-engined Racing Car, How to Build (Pashley)
Motorsport, Getting Started in (Collins)
Nissan GT-R High-performance Manual, The (Gorodji)
Nitrous Oxide High-performance Manual, The (Langfield)
Race & Trackday Driving Techniques (Hornsey)
Retro or classic car for high performance, How to modify your (Stapleton)
Rover V8 Engines, How to Power Tune (Hammill)
Secrets of Speed – Today's techniques for 4-stroke engine blueprinting & tuning (Swager)
Sportscar & Kitcar Suspension & Brakes, How to Build & Modify – Revised 3rd Edition (Hammill)
SU Carburettor High-performance Manual (Hammill)
Successful Low-Cost Rally Car, How to Build a (Young)
V8 Engine, How to Build a Short Block For High Performance (Hammill)
Weber DCOE, & Dellorto DHLA Carburetors, How to Build & Power Tune – 3rd Edition (Hammill)

Great Cars
Austin-Healey – A celebration of the fabulous 'Big' Healey (Piggott)
Jaguar E-type (Thorley)
Jaguar Mark 1 & 2 (Thorley)
Triumph TR – TR2 to 6: The last of the traditional sports cars (Piggott)

General
1½-litre GP Racing 1961-1965 (Whitelock)
Alfa Romeo 155/156/147 Competition Touring Cars (Collins)
Alfa Romeo Giulia Coupé GT & GTA (Tipler)
Alfa Romeo Montreal – The dream car that came true (Taylor)
Alfa Romeo Montreal – The Essential Companion (Classic Reprint of 500 copies) (Taylor)
Alfa Tipo 33 (McDonough & Collins)
Alpine & Renault – The Development of the Revolutionary Turbo F1 Car 1968 to 1979 (Smith)
Alpine & Renault – The Sports Prototypes 1963 to 1969 (Smith)
Alpine & Renault – The Sports Prototypes 1973 to 1978 (Smith)

An Incredible Journey (Falls & Reisch)
Anatomy of the Classic Mini (Huthert & Ely)
Anatomy of the Works Minis (Moylan)
Art Deco and British Car Design (Down)
Austin Cars 1948 to 1990 – a pictorial history (Rowe)
Autodrome (Collins & Ireland)
Automotive A-Z, Lane's Dictionary of Automotive Terms (Lane)
Automotive Mascots (Kay & Springate)
Bahamas Speed Weeks, The (O'Neil)
Bentley Continental, Corniche and Azure (Bennett)
Bentley MkVI, Rolls-Royce Silver Wraith, Dawn & Cloud/Bentley R & S-Series (Nutland)
BMC Competitions Department Secrets (Turner, Chambers & Browning)
BMW 5-Series (Cranswick)
BMW Z-Cars (Taylor)
BMW Cafe Racers (Cloesen)
BMW Classic 5 Series 1972 to 2003 (Cranswick)
BMW Custom Motorcycles – Choppers, Cruisers, Bobbers, Trikes & Quads (Cloesen)
BMW – The Power of M (Vivian)
British Cars, The Complete Catalogue of, 1895-1975 (Culshaw & Horrobin)
British Custom Motorcycles – The Brit Chop – choppers, cruisers, bobbers & trikes (Cloesen)
Bugatti – The 8-cylinder Touring Cars 1920-34 (Price & Arbey)
Carrera Panamericana, La (Tipler)
Car-tastrophes – 80 automotive atrocities from the past 20 years (Honest John, Fowler)
Chrysler 300 – America's Most Powerful Car 2nd Edition (Ackerson)
Chrysler PT Cruiser (Ackerson)
Cobra – The Real Thing! (Legate)
Competition Car Aerodynamics 3rd Edition (McBeath)
Competition Car Composites A Practical Handbook (Revised 2nd Edition) (McBeath)
Concept Cars, How to illustrate and design – New 2nd Edition (Dewey)
Cortina – Ford's Bestseller (Robson)
Cosworth – The Search for Power (6th edition) (Robson)
Coventry Climax Racing Engines (Hammill)
Daily Mirror 1970 World Cup Rally 40, The (Robson)
Dino – The V6 Ferrari (Long)
Dodge Challenger & Plymouth Barracuda (Grist)
Dodge Charger – Enduring Thunder (Ackerson)
Dodge Dynamite! (Grist)
Dune Buggy, Building A – The Essential Manual (Shakespeare)
Fast Ladies – Female Racing Drivers 1888 to 1970 (Bouzanquet)
Ferrari 288 GTO, The Book of the (Sackey)
Ferrari 333 SP (O'Neil)
Fiat & Abarth 124 Spider & Coupé (Tipler)
Fiat & Abarth 500 & 600 – 2nd Edition (Bobbitt)
Fiats, Great Small (Ward)
Fine Art of the Motorcycle Engine, The (Peirce)
Ford Cleveland 335-Series V8 engine 1970 to 1982 – The Essential Source Book (Hammill)
Ford F100/F150 Pick-up 1948-1996 (Ackerson)
Ford F150 Pick-up 1997-2005 (Ackerson)
Ford Focus WRC (Robson)
Ford GT – Then, and Now (Streather)
Ford GT40 (Legate)
Ford Midsize Muscle – Fairlane, Torino & Ranchero (Cranswick)
Ford Model Y (Roberts)
Ford Small Block V8 Racing Engines 1962-1970 – The Essential Source Book (Hammill)
Ford Thunderbird From 1954, The Book of the (Long)
Formula One - The Real Score? (Harvey)
Formula 5000 Motor Racing, Back then ... and back now (Lawson)
Forza Minardi! (Vigar)

Power, 1948-1980 (Pritchard)
Grand Prix Ford – DFV-powered Formula 1 Cars (Robson)
GT – The World's Best GT Cars 1953-73 (Dawson)
Hillclimbing & Sprinting – The Essential Manual (Short & Wilkinson)
How to Restore & Improve Classic Car Suspension, Steering & Wheels (Parish, translator)
Immortal Austin Seven (Morgan)
Inside the Rolls-Royce & Bentley Styling Department – 1971 to 2001 (Hull)
Jeep CJ (Ackerson)
Jeep Wrangler (Ackerson)
Karmann-Ghia Coupé & Convertible (Bobbitt)
Kris Meeke – Intercontinental Rally Challenge Champion (McBride)
Lamborghini Miura Bible, The (Sackey)
Lamborghini Urraco, The Book of the (Landsem)
Lancia 037 (Collins)
Lancia Delta HF Integrale (Blaettel & Wagner)
Lancia Delta Integrale (Collins)
Land Rover Series III Reborn (Porter)
Land Rover, The Half-ton Military (Cook)
Lea-Francis Story, The (Price)
Le Mans Panoramic (Ireland)
Maserati 250F In Focus (Pritchard)
Mazda MX-5 Miata, the book of the – The 'Mk1' NA-series 1988 to 1997 (Long)
Mazda MX-5 Miata Roadster (Long)
Mazda Rotary-engined Cars (Cranswick)
Maximum Mini (Booij)
Meet the English (Bowie)
MGA (Price Williams)
MGB & MGB GT– Expert Guide (Auto-doc Series) (Williams)
MGB Electrical Systems Updated & Revised Edition (Astley)
Micro Caravans (Jenkinson)
Micro Trucks (Mort)
Microcars at Large! (Quellin)
Mini Cooper – The Real Thing! (Tipler)
Mini Minor to Asia Minor (West)
Mitsubishi Lancer Evo, The Road Car & WRC Story (Long)
Montlhéry, The Story of the Paris Autodrome (Boddy)
Moto Guzzi Sport & Le Mans Bible, The (Falloon)
The Moto Guzzi Story - 3rd Edition (Falloon)
Motor Movies – The Posters! (Veysey)
Motor Racing – Reflections of a Lost Era (Carter)
Motor Racing – The Pursuit of Victory 1930-1962 (Carter)
Motor Racing – The Pursuit of Victory 1963-1972 (Wyatt/Sears)
Motor Racing Heroes – The Stories of 100 Greats (Newman)
Motorcycle Road & Racing Chassis Designs (Noakes)
Motorsport In colour, 1950s (Wainwright)
N.A.R.T. – A concise history of the North American Racing Team 1957 to 1983 (O'Neil)
Nissan 300ZX & 350Z – The Z-Car Story (Long)
Nissan GT-R Supercar: Born to race (Gorodji)
Northeast American Sports Car Races 1950-1959 (O'Neil)
Norton Commando Bible – All models 1968 to 1978 (Henshaw)
Nothing Runs – Misadventures in the Classic, Collectable & Exotic Car Biz (Slutsky)
Pontiac Firebird – New 3rd Edition (Cranswick)
Porsche 356 (2nd Edition) (Long)
Porsche 908 (Födisch, Neßhöver, Roßbach, Schwarz & Roßbach)
Porsche 911 Carrera – The Last of the Evolution (Corlett)
Porsche 911R, RS & RSR, 4th Edition (Starkey)
Porsche 911, The Book of the (Long)
Porsche 911 – The Definitive History 2004-2012 (Long)
Porsche – The Racing 914s (Smith)

Companion (Streather)
Porsche 914 & 914-6: The Definitive History of the Road & Competition Cars (Long)
Porsche 924 (Long)
The Porsche 924 Carreras – evolution to excellence (Smith)
Porsche Racing Cars – 1953 to 1975 (Long)
Porsche Racing Cars – 1976 to 2005 (Long)
Porsche – The Rally Story (Meredith)
Porsche: Three Generations of Genius (Meredith)
Powered by Porsche (Smith)
RAC Rally Action! (Gardiner)
Rallye Sport Fords: The Inside Story (Moreton)
Rolls-Royce Silver Shadow/Bentley T Series Corniche & Camargue – Revised & Enlarged Edition (Bobbitt)
Rolls-Royce Silver Spirit, Silver Spur & Bentley Mulsanne 2nd Edition (Bobbitt)
Rootes Cars of the 50s, 60s & 70s – Hillman, Humber, Singer, Sunbeam & Talbot (Rowe)
Rover P4 (Bobbitt)
Runways & Racers (O'Neil)
RX-7 – Mazda's Rotary Engine Sportscar (Updated & Revised New Edition) (Long)
Singer Story: Cars, Commercial Vehicles, Bicycles & Motorcycle (Atkinson)
Sleeping Beauties USA – abandoned classic cars & trucks (Marek)
SM – Citroën's Maserati-engined Supercar (Long & Claverol)
Speedway – Auto racing's ghost tracks (Collins & Ireland)
Supercar, How to Build your own (Thompson)
Tales from the Toolbox (Oliver)
Tatra – The Legacy of Hans Ledwinka, Updated & Enlarged Collector's Edition of 1500 copies (Margolius & Henry)
This Day in Automotive History (Corey)
To Boldly Go – twenty six vehicle designs that dared to be different (Hull)
Toyota Celica & Supra, The Book of Toyota's Sports Coupés (Long)
Toyota MR2 Coupés & Spyders (Long)
TT Talking – The TT's most exciting era – As seen by Manx Radio TT's lead commentator 2004-2012 (Lambert)
Two Summers – The Mercedes-Benz W196R Racing Car (Ackerson)
TWR Story, The – Group A (Hughes & Scott)
Unraced (Collins)
Velocette Motorcycles – MSS to Thruxton – New Third Edition (Burris)
Vespa – The Story of a Cult Classic in Pictures (Uhlig)
Vincent Motorcycles: The Untold Story since 1946 (Guyony & Parker)
Volkswagens of the World (Glen)
VW Beetle Cabriolet – The full story of the convertible Beetle (Bobbitt)
VW Beetle – The Car of the 20th Century (Copping)
VW Golf: Five Generations of Fun (Copping & Cservenka)
VW – The Air-cooled Era (Copping)
VW T5 Camper Conversion Manual (Porter)
VW Campers (Copping)
Volkswagen Type 3, The book of the – Concept, Design, International Production Models & Development (Glen)
Volvo Estate, The (Hollebone)
You & Your Jaguar XK8/XKR – Buying, Enjoying, Maintaining, Modifying – New Edition (Thorley)
Which Oil? – Choosing the right oils & greases for your antique, vintage, veteran, classic or collector car (Michell)
Wolseley Cars 1948 to 1975 (Rowe)
Works Minis, The Last (Purves & Brenchley)
Works Rally Mechanic (Moylan)

www.veloce.co.uk

First published in March 2019 by Veloce Publishing Limited, Veloce House, Parkway Farm Business Park, Middle Farm Way, Poundbury, Dorchester DT1 3AR, England.
Fax 01305 250479 / Tel 01305 260068 / e-mail info@veloce.co.uk / web www.veloce.co.uk or www.velocebooks.com.
ISBN: 978-1-787112-67-4 UPC: 6-36847-01267-0

The "Big Bird" Thunderbird still offered full-size pizzazz until the end of 1976. However, Lee Iacocca rightly predicted America's changing taste for downsized personal luxury, that made the 1974 Mustang II such a great commercial success. (Courtesy Ford Motor Co)

Contents

Foreword by John H Davis – Host and creator of *MotorWeek*

The year was 1970, and boy do I remember it well. That was the year I graduated from college, having earned a BS in Mechanical/Aerospace Engineering from North Carolina State University. Unfortunately, the winding down of the Vietnam War had curtailed the need for new flying war machines, and the fledgling engineers that might cut their teeth designing them. Plus, the economy as a whole was on a downward tilt after barely surviving the tumultuous 1960s. Inflation was on the rise, as was unemployment, along with budget and trade deficits, as the American attitudes about themselves were falling into a funk.

It was into this market Ford Motor Company introduced the rear-wheel drive Pinto, the first subcompact class car Ford had ever made in America. The official unveiling was September 11, 1970. That first Pinto was a product of its times. Rushed to the market by then Ford Executive Vice President Lee Iacocca, the Pinto fulfilled his desire for a small, lightweight, inexpensive car that answered the demands of a populous who no longer saw America as the world's unchallengeable economic giant. Iacocca didn't have to be the marketing genius he was to read the tea leaves of increasing pressure on gas prices, tightening tailpipe emissions, new safety standards, and the growing popularity of small imported cars. He clearly understood the urgency of Detroit providing vehicles that embraced, rather than fought, the new realities of the American car market.

So, what happened? Well, the Pinto was by most accounts a home run. In its first model year some 350,000 units were sold, with nearly 500,000 sales for the 1972 model year. The Pinto stayed in production for ten model years with total production of sedans, hatchbacks, and wagons of over 3 million units. With so many used Pintos available at bargain basement prices, no wonder it was a popular choice for amateur racers well into the 1990s.

But, by 1973, things were already starting to go wrong for the Pinto, as reports of cars bursting into flames after collisions spread throughout the media. When the Pinto was designed, government crash criteria for rear-end collisions were still in flux. Placing the gas tank at the back, between the rear differential and the bumper, was common practice for many global carmakers. Still, the smaller size of the Pinto, as well as some other shortsighted engineering decisions, seemed to make it more prone to cataclysmic accidents. By the time it was determined that it was no more likely to catch fire in a rear-end collision than many other cars of its time, the damage was done to the Pinto, as well as to the reputation of American car design quality.

Into this same deteriorating environment, the Ford Mustang II was introduced for 1974. Sharing its platform with the Pinto, the Mustang II's design mimicked Ford's original pony car, which had shared its underpinning with the compact Falcon. But, the first gen Mustang had grown too big for many of its buyers, and the 'II' was the solution. Indeed, despite most Mustang fans, including myself, looking down on the stubby second generation car, it sold very well. The 1974 Mustang II racked up over 385,000 units, or almost three times the sales of the outgoing 1973 Mustang. No doubt, the 1973 oil embargo that coincided with the car's launch had a lot to do with its initial success.

Looking back on both the Pinto and the Mustang II, one can make the case that both foretold the downsizing of cars that would accelerate in the 1980s. But to me, they were both examples of rapidly changing automotive attitudes by the public and thus Detroit. No longer could the 'Big 3' dictate car design in a vacuum. Social pressures, conservationism, the now instantaneous coverage by television, and of course, the continuing of the rising import car tide, all required a faster response from Detroit, even if the outcome was less than perfect.

In particular, the Pinto's checkered history, quality issues, along with import concerns, likely prompted Ford to look offshore for a more advanced replacement. That would be the European designed, front-wheel drive 1981 Ford Escort; its self-proclaimed 'World Car.' Which, as it so happens, was the first car we tested on *MotorWeek* when we went on the air in October of that same year. It was obvious to us at first drive that the Escort was a far better car than the Pinto could ever aspire to be.

In the end, the Ford Pinto and Ford Mustang II were not able to curtail imported car popularity, and the Pinto clearly fostered even tougher safety regulations. But, without them, and other domestic small car attempts of that era like the AMC Gremlin, Chevrolet Vega, and even the Mitsubishi made Dodge Colt, the fortunes of Detroit automakers would have been even worse during the 1970s than they were. For good and for bad, the 1971 Ford Pinto and the 1974 Ford Mustang II were cars that were exactly what that period in our American history demanded.

John H Davis

Introduction – Dearborn discovers small cars

In the beginning Lee Iacocca created the Mustang, and the world judged that it was good. Ten years hence the world was in trouble, and once again Big Lee and Mustang came forth. In troubled times of rising insurance premiums, gas prices and inflation, Henry's Mustang II rose to the occasion with aplomb.

Between the demise of the original Mustang and the coming of Foxstang, the Mustang II carried Henry's inimitable nameplate when rivals had bitten the dust. No one has ever won a drag race by intentionally skipping second gear!

As Ford's pony car standard bearer, Mustang II got attention from customizers and supplied hardware to hotrodders. The downsized pony won on the track and in the showroom, adding over 1 million to the Mustang tally. It didn't always win approval from pony car fans, being distinctly different from earlier Mustangs. It was also related to a controversial subcompact called Pinto.

Ford Pinto was Henry's small car rival to the VW Beetle, Datsun and Toyota. Along with Vega and Gremlin, the Pinto represented an era when Detroit took on the imports, before relying on back door imports and the truck/SUV market. The Pinto sold over 3 million copies, and provided reliable, economical ownership for many. Like Mustang II, it was also a trackside winner. Unfortunately, Pinto also picked up some largely undeserved auto safety accusations.

The 1970s brought many challenges for Ford, Detroit and car enthusiasts. Could car fans survive world events, lobby groups, federal regulations and still find fun small cars? Mustang II and Pinto could help. They were interesting times and like the ad said: 'Mustang II Boredom Zero.' Cheers, Henry!

Marc Cranswick

A brave new world

"That car looks like 100mph parked at the curb," said a passer-by to Bud Lindemann. The comment concerned a new 1969 Mustang 428 Cobra Jet, a coupe that was no shrinking violet. However, in 1974 with fuel crisis gas lines lengthening, where did all that street machismo get you? The Allstate insurance man liked you, your premiums were paying for his early retirement. Saudi Arabia was also a big fan. Insuring and feeding Dearborn's big-block bolide helped both their causes, but not yours.

By 1973, Ford's Mustang was a success – it had sold over 3 million steeds since April 1964 – but it was a success in trouble. What started out as a lithe, small-block V8 pony car of moderate size had morphed into something mainstream buyers didn't want anymore. As with other pony cars (the genre Lee Iacocca and Don Frey started), the Mustang got faster, but it also got heavier and less economical.

personal cars and subcompacts, but not pony or muscle cars. Pony cars had been on a sales decline since the start of 1968. Lee Iacocca could see the writing on the wall long before the first Mustang fell to just 134,867 annual sales.

When presiding over the new upscale Granada/Monarch compacts, Iacocca said a guy would no longer buy a car just because it had a long hood. Big Lee took that new age thinking to senior Ford management, as early as November 1969. A new kind of car was needed to attract sales. With overall qualities Detroit had heretofore ignored, Ford was about to challenge the imports in the small economy car class. However, Mustang's new mission lay upscale of that, with the Arizona Project.

The imports had garnered increasing market share with a new type of luxury car. It was well-made and easy to drive and park, thanks to small external dimensions. Such cars weren't overly ostentatious, or very powerful, but they

Left: On debut in late 1973, the new Mustang II Ghia attracted a lot of positive public attention. Styling was by Lincoln-Mercury division. (Courtesy www.grautogallery.com)

The whole pony car corral had been getting more expensive to buy, insure and feed. For a time – 1965 to 1968 – this was fine, and buyers couldn't get enough. However, rising premiums, falling horsepower from federal pollution controls, and a weary consumer looking for something new ended the good times. By 1973 domestic buyers were favoring sporty luxo intermediate

offered sporty refinement to a number of American buyers who hadn't been catered to. Such people went to Mercedes for their Compact, or Volvo for a 142S, or even one of the upscale Japanese coupes. Indeed, Ford had just such a car in their family: the Mercury Capri.

The Capri was a product of Ford Europe. It was that continent's answer to the Mustang. A svelte coupe with rack

Right: On '74 MY release, Mustang II offered the 2.8-liter Cologne V6 as a $229 option. However, this 1977 Mustang II Ghia has the popular 302 V8. (Courtesy www.grautogallery.com)

and pinion steering and smooth, revvable 2.6 V6 motor. It was billed as 'The Sexy European.' Basically, Catherine Spaak in car form, or was that the mid-engined Italian Pantera? Cadillac must have been green with envy as the Capri and Pantera dropped the average age of Lincoln-Mercury dealer visitors by decades. In spite of exchange rate revaluations, and being sold through a fuddy duddy dealer network, the Capri and Pantera sold well. They dominated their North American niches. For a time there was only one European import that outsold the Capri: the VW Beetle!

The 'Right Time' Ford

The Capri and Pantera were great for Americans looking for a European car, but now Ford wanted an American designed and built car, with European qualities. America's answer to the Capri. That's the car the Arizona Project would become: the Mustang II – the 'Right Time' Ford. In the aftermath of the 1973 Arab-Israeli war, OPEC decided the world had been paying too little for oil, and so quadrupled its price overnight.

Supply shortages over the winter of 1973/74 made smaller, thriftier rides desirable, and Henry had one ready with Mustang II. The original Falcon-based Mustang was 181in long, 68.2in wide and rode on a 108in wheelbase. Adventurous, marketing-driven styling saw this first generation puff out to respective dimensions of 189.5in, 74.1in and 109in.

Mustang II cut those figures to 175in, 70in and 96.6in for length, width and wheelbase respectively. For gas mileage comparison, *Autocar*'s May 25 1974 issue compared the final '73 Mustang Grande V8 automatic with the new '74 Mustang II Ghia V6 automatic. It was 15.1mpg versus 20.5mpg in favor of the new car. In a fuel crisis, mileage mattered.

The 1973 Mustang's sales total was pretty disappointing, given 1973 had been a big sales year for the auto industry. With the fuel crisis and ensuing inflationary pressures, depressed economic times saw a 1974 sales slide for most segments. It was all down, just a question of degree. The first half of 1974 witnessed a 25% sales decline for Ford Pinto, and Vega fell 13%. Chevy Nova and Ford Maverick posted declines of 13% and 21%, respectively. However, the bigger they are, the harder they fall. Compared to an average industry decline of 24% during the first half of 1974, full-size domestic sales declined 50%.[1]

Ford Galaxie could thank those police fleet sales. Law enforcement generally stayed loyal to full-size for space, power and durability. However, the rest were looking for something smaller. In the economy car ranks, Plymouth Valiant scored an 18% sales rise. Luxury and upscale cars also seemed more recession resilient. Mercedes and other big buck imports always seemed to weather the storm. So did the 1974 Mustang II. Even without a V8 option – a first in Mustang

history and never repeated – Mustang II powered on to 385,993 sales. There was also a lot of advertising, just like ten years earlier. You can lead a horse to water, and thankfully Mustang II drank!

Engineering –
all in the Ford family

The basis behind Ford's winning new luxury subcompact was the Ford Pinto. Pinto's big brother Maverick represented a reworking of Falcon's chassis design. With space at a premium, a direct interpretation wasn't possible with Pinto and Mustang II. However, SLA (short long arm) front suspension and leaf sprung live axle were reminiscent of Henry's 1960 compact, and alien to a 1981 Ford Escort. Nevertheless, in keeping with Mustang II's upscale nature, many refinements were made versus Pinto. The Mustang II's unibody utilized front independent suspension with upper A-arms and lower lateral arms. There were also compliance struts, tube shocks and a swaybar.

The front coils lived between the suspension's control arms, unlike the original Mustang. This compact affair got rid of the spring towers, freeing up underhood space for the Blue Oval's 302 V8! A little car with a Big Car Ride – that was the engineers' aim. To this end the front subframe that motor and transmission were mounted to had six rubber insulated mounts. The subframe was attached to the front crossmember. Rubber mounts molded and bonded with paint shop heat, as Mustang II rolled along the assembly line.

The front subframe's axial strut was connected between the lower suspension arm and the subframe. This permitted the front wheels to move slightly rearwards when a bump was struck, reducing NVH. Brake dive was minimized by tilting the balljoints and upper A-arms. At the rear, Hotchkiss type live axle with leafs were similar building blocks as seen on Falcon, Mustang One et al, but now with more refinement. Rubber bushings meant no metal to metal contact. The rubber isoclamp muffled leaf spring and hangar action when locating the live axle.

Autocar magazine sampled an automatic '75 Mustang II Ghia V8 hardtop on the imperfect surfaces of Britain. They said the front subframe

The plush Ghia interior was a $96 option on base notchback and hatchback Mustang IIs. Zombie shift V8 power teams employed the C4 automatic. (Courtesy www.grautogallery.com)

insulators and rear isoclamp spring encaser prevented bumps from reaching car occupants. The Pinto and Mustang II shared subframe and suspension parts, much like Falcon and Mustang One had done. However, the whole was greater than the sum of the parts. Ford engineer Bob Negstad had developed effective chassis hardware for successful IMSA circle track Pinto racers. Ford Pinto became the first volume-produced domestic car with rack and pinion steering. Naturally, this system was passed on to Mustang II. This promised greater steering response than that offered by the original Mustang's recirculating ball setup. The rack and pinion system was bolted to the front suspension crossmember. The steering system was mounted using three pads to further cut NVH. Steering ratios were 24:1 and 19:1 for the respective non-power and power racks. The latter cut lock to lock work from 4.2 to 3.3 turns. As with most domestics, power assist was practically mandatory to overcome unwieldy and heavy work when Mustang II's optional V6 and V8s were specified.

Moving with the times, Mustang II came with standard front disk brakes sized 9.3in, and accompanied by 9in rear drums. For a sub 3000lb car they were adequate, but not generous. A limiting factor was Mustang II's 13in rims. All examples had a four-bolt 4.25in pattern. However, braking saw an objective improvement over Mustang One. *Motor Trend* compared an original 289 V8 car with a new Mustang II V8 in November 1974. Judging 30-0mph and 60-0mph stops, it was the younger steed that prevailed. Respective stopping distances were 35 versus 32ft, and 172 versus 147ft. However, back in the '60s, car fans were more concerned with going, not stopping!

Design & styling

When you are the model that started the fashion-conscious pony car genre, design and styling is a big deal. The Mustang II's production design was set as early as 1971 by Dick Nesbitt. Lee Iacocca had taken over from Bunkie Knudsen as FoMoCo President on December 10 1970. He wasted no time saving Mustang by directing its new trailblazing downsized form. Iacocca wasn't happy with Knudsen's reign, when the once-sporty pony was allowed to bloat out

Even though Lima 2.3 and Cologne V6 were struggling with smog laws, the two-barrel 302 V8 was gaining ground during 1975-79. By '77 MY torque was up to 242lb/ft, and CR had risen to 8.4:1. DuraSpark ignition was standard on FoMoCo powerplants. (Courtesy www.grautogallery.com)

virtually to Torino size in the early '70s. All accompanied by a sales slide into oblivion.

Even so, Mustang II looked awfully familiar. So too the established notchback and fastback formats. Iacocca had asked for both, but there were changes from the first Mustang. Although the new notchback was marketed as a hardtop, it actually had a concealed B-pillar. A concession to feared rollover federal roof strength testing. The hatchback format was rising in popularity. The new Capri MkII and other imports had the versatile feature. Traditional ponies had limited luggage capacity.

One needed the optional trunk-mounted luggage rack to strap down a toothbrush! Now, Mustang II could serve as a small family car. Trunk space was 9.6ft^3, and a huge 18ft^3 when the hatchback's rear pews were sleeping. The entry level hatch was basically a two-seater with luggage platform, a business coupe for the '70s, if you will. Ford called it their first two-seater car since the '57 Thunderbird. The 2+2 and upscale Mach I fastbacks were delivered with a standard fold-down rear seat. It was an option on notchback.

Mustang II's styling was the result of a four-way competition. It was a fight out between the departments of Ford, Lincoln-Mercury, Advanced Design and the recently acquired Italian styling house of Ghia. The last entity was associated with Chrysler Corp dream cars of the '50s. Lincoln-Mercury won out. This was apt since it sold the car, Capri, that Mustang II was supposed to emulate with American flavor. Fittingly, Mustang II was very home-grown, and looked like a Mustang also. Many car journals picked up on Mustang II continuing the American tradition of curved sheetmetal muscle, as opposed to the fashionable sleek wedges of Europe.

Britain's *Autocar* magazine noted the new steed's attractive, sporting style was definitely not European. The journal also saw great similarity between the new Ghia hardtop and the classic 1964 ½ Mustang notchback. From its April 1975 report: "Lines are reminiscent of the original 1965 Mustang." Indeed, objectively Mustang II was the last Mustang to look like a Mustang, until the retro fifth-gen pony galloped into view for 2006 MY. Generations three and four were modern contemporary designs.

The sight most commonly seen by I4 and 262ci Chebby Monzas! Amber turn signals were a classy European touch. (Courtesy www.grautogallery.com)

Ford Mustang II & Pinto

Here, Ford increasingly added styling cues from the 'good 'ol days,' to remind new Mustang buyers of their steed's heritage.

It was that new notchback, the 1974 Mustang II hardtop, that garnered initial attention on Mainstreet USA, and it was two thumbs up from the public. In December 1973, *Motor Trend*'s Jim Brokaw mentioned that drivers asked "how much?" One even said the Ghia hardtop looked like the sinfully expensive Mercedes 450SL, AKA 'The Beverly Hills Golf Cart.' This last observation kind of got history backwards. The 1971-89 R107 Mercedes was a personal car that took styling influence from the original 1964 ½ Ford Mustang. Henry got there first!

In 1977, *Road Test* received similar enquiries and appreciative glances when testing the '70s Mazda Cosmo coupe. It seemed the public really dug the mini sports/luxo personal car route. Coupes like the Mustang II Ghia, Chevy Monza and Cosmo were the next step after the sports/luxo midsizers known as Monte Carlo and Matador Coupe. It showed the tremendous foresight of Lee Iacocca, putting Ford on the sales race pole position with Mustang II. However, the new '74 MY fastback made less of an initial impression.

Jim Brokaw put fastback's low profile down to the numerous nature of sporty small cars. Apart from stock Mercury Capris, Opel Rallyes, and Celicas, there were also modified Datsuns, captive-import Colts, Crickets, domestic Vegas and Pintos. All lowered, with sports exhaust systems. Such enthusiasm was also bestowed on the small car that started it all, Herbie the VW!

Mustang II hardtop had a distinct Torino-era Formal Roof, to distinguish itself from the madding four-cylinder crowd. However, the Mustang II fastback was considered too visually close to the Pinto, even in Mach I guise. Brokaw felt this was the reason his Mach I steed was getting fewer eye candy glances. If that was the outside story, inside Mustang II had few class equals. In 1972 *Road & Track* sampled a Mercedes 280SEL 4.5 V8, nearly 11 grand with power sunroof. Quality was as expected, except for the trunk. This 17ft³ space was no better finished or trimmed than a plain American intermediate. However, Mustang II's trunk was a class above.

With the rear seat folded down, *Road & Track* found a fully cut pile carpeted load area of greater volume. Padded vinyl complimented non-carpeted parts. There were no exposed metal surfaces. The spare was under carpet, not exposed like in the Benz, and gas-filled struts kept the hatch open. It was a safe place to stow handmade Italian leather luggage, which would have been at home in the optional

Ghia interior package, costing $96 on the 1974 Mach I. This environment, seen most commonly on Mustang II Ghia hardtop, was praised almost universally.

Autocar judged the Ghia hardtop to have a nice luxury interior: "… the simulated wood panels on the door trims look very good." In contrast, Steve Spence of *Motor Trend* described Chevy Monza's friends of the forest as: "… paper-thin screw-down junk …" Only GM's bean counters were pleased. The sole reservation concerning Ghia hardtop's interior was expressed by Herb L Adams of *Motor Trend* in August 1975. Even though such Ghia luxury accoutrements were commensurate with this class of car, Adams said the boudoir décor was a challenge to the staff's masculinity.

Compared to Pinto, Ford wisely ponied up a unique interior design for Mustang II. There was the exception of the steering wheel. However, come 1976 and the Chevy Corvette purloined its tiller from the humble Vega. Ford revised the Mustang II's steering wheel for 1975. The dashboard was an upscale hooded nacelle molding, with wood or brushed metal inlays on instrument surrounds, and passenger trim panel above the glovebox. Ghia specified cars had a digital clock inlaid into the latter trim panel.

Thanks to lots of sound insulation, no roof gutters and chassis rubber mounts,

Mustang II lived up to the old Rolls-Royce saying – 'the loudest sound at 60mph was the clock!' Trim inlays continued on door cards in faux walnut or brushed metal. The rocker panels had cover plates and there was thick pile carpet underfoot. Buckets were standard in all Mustang IIs, and possessed full-width headrests. The front seats were deeply coved, to provide some relief for rear seat passengers. Between said buckets lay a European style handbrake – a Mustang first.

Ghia and sporty models came with circular tach and speedo, left to right. There were three smaller round gages for gas, battery charge and coolant temp to the right. Only the absence of an oil pressure gage denied full instrumentation. However, upscale Euromobiles did no better. *Road & Track* noted the presence of European door armrests, like a BMW. Ghia trim also brought softer grade vinyl, with buttons and a block pattern for rear seating. Accent stripes for the front buckets were color-matched to the exterior.

It was an era when vinyl looked like real leather, only lacking that authentic hide scent. The cloth edition was similarly plush, and carried an equivalent button pattern. There were no seat heaters in this era, but Ford had HVAC matters well in hand. Swing out rear windows on the hatchback, optional steel sliding

Below left: As a modification, this 1978 Mustang II Ghia's C4 auto deals with a 1990 roller 5.0 HO V8. (Courtesy www.forgottenpony.com)

Below right: Keeping things color coordinated, this Ghia's Aqua half vinyl roof is color matched to an Aqua two tone interior. (Courtesy www.forgottenpony.com)

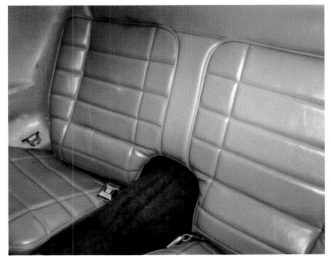

sunroof, or pricier one-way glass Moonroof. The latter could be flipped open at the rear, or removed completely.

With the 1970 Boss Mustang, only one car built had factory a/c. This white Boss 302 also had factory 8-track player fitted. All a custom order for a Ford executive. Relatively few sporty cars, or cars in general, up to the early '70s had factory a/c fitted. The systems were an expensive option, and many buyers just regarded a/c as more money. Not much use in the snowbelt, but times were changing.

1973 was the last year for a factory Mustang ragtop, until its 1983 return. Feared federal rollover testing, and changing buyer tastes towards a more refined, closed interior, saw factory a/c become a more common option. *Consumer Reports* harrumphed over 1971 Mustang's lack of moveable vent grilles. However, many Mustang IIs came with factory a/c – an effective, neatly integrated system, which had two extra dash vent grilles. Non a/c cars had fresh air grilles at the dashboard's extreme ends. An air-conditioned Mustang II had one more grille above the temp gage, and one to the left of the Ghia's digital clock.

In 1974, a/c was the Mustang II's single priciest option at $368. It all went with an interior American car buyers

wanted, very plush and extremely hush. Apart from remarks concerning Mustang II having greater ride refinement than Pinto, it was universally judged as being very quiet. There were facts present to affirm the assertion. *Road Test*'s April '75 report on a Mustang II Mach I 302 automatic revealed 71dBA at 70mph. *Road & Track*'s May '78 reading for the Jaguar XJ12L was 72dBA. This regal V12 bastion of refinement cost over 19 grand; Dearborn's delight was under 7k in 1978. In the future Dearborn would own Browns Lane, in some ways it already did!

Not everyone wants to race around in an insanely loud fastback, wearing a black turtleneck. For the majority of Americans, Mustang II permitted hours of US gray flannel interstate, to be dispatched with climate-controlled comfort. Quiet enough to enjoy the dulcet tones of Engelbert Humperdinck on FM radio. Henry offered a factory-fit AM/FM stereo receiver for 213 bones. *Motor Trend*'s Jim Brokaw noted that the Mustang II Mach I V6 easily dealt with the Santa Ana freeway's hop-inducing surface.

Indeed, there seemed much to commend about the new Mustang II. From an optional overhead console maplight, to many detail design

This completely standard, original condition 1978 Mustang II Ghia V8 is called Snow White. Snow White has only had mild restoration work. (Courtesy Tony Hall)

refinements. It was a car with practical driving in mind. After years of fantasy, Mustang II's real world luxury contrasted with Edsel's showmanship. Little wonder *Motor Trend* chose the Mustang II as its 1974 Car of the Year. A frequent remark from the independent press was that Mustang II behaved like a baby Lincoln Mk IV. A comfortable highway cruiser that cocooned its occupants, disturbed only by a distant V8 hum on 302-optioned cars.

There was truth to the Mustang II's insulating nature. Ford chief engineer Stuart M Frey, younger brother of Mustang One's co-creator Don Frey, said that Lee Iacocca wanted Mustang II to have a high standard of fit and finish. He wanted Ford's new pony to be "a little jewel." So Mustang II was going to be different from its Mercury Capri sibling. That coupe was sports luxury, whereas many versions of Mustang II were luxury sports. To make the jump from selling tens of thousands to hundreds of thousands, that was a distinction Mustang II made as it appealed to mainstream tastes.

The stats explained the different nature of the Capri and its US counterpart. Comparing final 2.3-liter four-cylinder versions of Mustang II, and also hatchback Capri II, respective length, width, height and weight were 175/70.2/50.3in and 2710lb versus 174.8/64.8/51in and 2590lb. Mustang II catered to the domestic buyer preference for more interior width. The extra girth meant less nimble road manners, and less acceleration for a given powerplant. *Road & Track* tested like-engined Mustang II Mach I and Capri 2800 V6s in January 1974. Respective summary figures for 0-60mph/ braking from 80mph/skidpad reading/ overall mpg/dBA at 70mph were 13.8 seconds/283ft/0.683/16.5mpg/75dBA versus 10.8 seconds/282ft/0.726/20mpg /79dBA. Understandably, the four-speed Mach I approximated its US market nemesis, the automatic 262ci Chevy Monza 2+2, much more closely. The Chebby's respective figures were 13.4 seconds/320ft/0.675/17mpg/74dBA, although this car was meeting the tighter 1975 emissions regulations.

The penalty for Mustang II's fastback style, was reduced rear headroom. However, the convenience of a hatchback and the V8 option added practicality and punch! (Courtesy Marc Cranswick)

In either case, it showed that these European-flavored American cars were plusher, quieter coupes with lower handling limits. Their higher weight made for poorer gas mileage, which would have become poorer still with more powerful V8 engines to match the Capri's scat. Car design has always been about trade-offs. Many US buyers wouldn't have cared much for the Capri's more spartan trim, and vocal V6.

Road & Track magazine favored the Capri's approach. This made sense given it was a small car advocate, with a history of dealing with European car evaluation. *Consumer Reports* even took the AMC Gremlin's side over Mustang II, in choosing an optimal subcompact. It seemed like Mustang II had less appeal to those with VW Beetle-type utilitarian leanings.

Mustang II power – waiting for a V8

The Mustang's horse logo was redesigned for Mustang II. The latest pony adorning the grille had changed its gait, from a gallop to a canter. The cynical would say it was symbolic of the declining performance of the country, FoMoCo and Mustang during difficult times. In truth, Ford was just providing power teams fitting for the subcompact class. To compete with Chevy Vega's

durability-troubled aluminum block 2.3-liter inline four, Henry had his Lima 2.3-liter four-pot, with cast iron block and head.

The Lima made its debut in the 1974 Ford Pinto, Capri and Mustang II. It was Ford's first all metric dimension motor. The Lima was a development of the 2-liter Pinto inline four. The motor that took its name from the American subcompact it was designed for. Used extensively in Ford's global empire, it made 100 horses in Euro spec, and 220bhp in Ford Escort rally cars. The larger Lima took its name from the Ford Lima Ohio factory it was made in. It was part of many firsts for the Mustang in 1974. The Mustang II was the first Mustang with standard front disk brakes, and four on the floor. To the chagrin of many Ford fans, it was also the first four-banger Stang!

Rated at 88 horse at five grand and 116lb/ft at 2600rpm, this hydraulic lifter five main bearing motor was no ball of fire, and breathed through a modest Holley two-barrel carb. However, it did its job as a reliable gasoline sipper. It was a post fuel crisis Secretary Special par excellence. A base $2895 two-door hardtop was no poverty mobile. With sensible options, $110 radials, $59 AM radio and 36 buck bumper guards, *Motor Trend* thought this was economy car daily driving at its best. The light Lima even saved on the expense of power steering. Ford's better idea on wheels for inflationary times.

One could team up the 140ci I4 with standard German Hummer four-speed, or Ford's C3 autobox. The latter was made in Bordeaux, France. The successful Mercury Capri had made its debut with the 2-liter overhead-cam Pinto I4, before offering the German Cologne 2.6 V6 OHV job for 1972. A smooth, lively V6 that liked to rev. A revised version of the Cologne V6 became Capri's and Mustang II's optional motor for '74 MY. Ford made changes to the 2.6 V6 for '74 due to emissions regs. It now displaced 2.8 liters, and was rated at a modest net 105bhp at 4600rpm, and 140lb/ft at 3200rpm.

Normally, T-tops were limited to the Mustang II fastback of 1977-78. However, this '78 hardtop V8 is a custom job by Tony Hall. Stumpy's Subframe Connectors help stiffen the structure for the '90 5.0 HO 4bbl V8. The 13x5in factory sport steel rims, wear B F Goodrich T/A radials. (Courtesy Tony Hall)

The new 2.8 Cologne V6 utilized the outgoing 2.6 motor's camshaft, valvetrain conrods and distributor. However, boring and stroking to get 2.8 liters necessitated a new block to be cast. The 2.8 V6 was standard Mach I fare, and a $229 option elsewhere. It could be teamed with the C3 autobox, or a US-built Borg Warner four-speed. Both the Lima and Cologne four-speeds had aluminum cases, and direct one to one top gears. Release info from Ford stated a 3.55 rear axle ratio for all North American Mustang IIs. On Lima and Cologne motors, the four-speed ratios were 3.65 (1st), 1.97 (2nd), 1.37 (3rd) and 1.00 (4th).

Come 1979 model year, the 2.3 Lima received a turbocharger and 132 horses. This output climbed to 205bhp with duals, a different turbo and fuel-injection. All courtesy of SVO's (Special Vehicle Operation) 1985 Mustang. Both powerplants live outside the Mustang II's era, but enthusiast hotrodders always consider retrofits! The Cologne V6 in 1974 Mustang II Mach I also came with duals and some build-up potential. The latter topic was covered by John Christy in the 1974 February issue of *Motor Trend*. The secret was good old-fashioned dyno tuning – still doable on a 1974 federal smogger, albeit with fewer returns compared to earlier times.

As recently as 1973, the Capri's 2.6 V6 was willing to visit 6500rpm, but now the 2.8 V6 surrendered at five grand. The emissions control effects were experienced by *Motor Trend*'s Mach I four-speed at Irwindale Raceway. There was wheelspin when dropping the clutch into first, and a chirp powershifting into second, but the 8.2:1 CR V6 had zero pulling power higher in the rev range. The new, more sophisticated 2.8 edition cylinder head was of little help. As with most engines passing the stricter smog test, the answer was lean carburetion. Trying to get the engine to run hotter and burn the fuel/air mix more thoroughly.

Mods run to a dual cold air intake, dual Flow Master exhaust, King Cobra snake hood graphic, and Ghia Sports Appearance Group. (Courtesy Tony Hall)

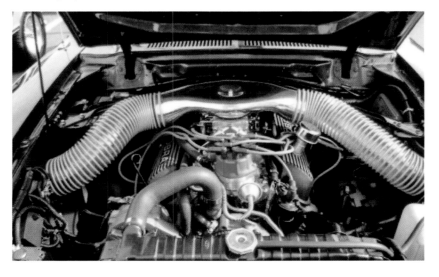

The 1974 V6 behaved none too shabbily. It started first time, hot or cold, and had a progressive choke action. However, there was stumbling at low speed, and even when the engine was warmed up. John Christy's dyno tune tips could help. To deal with the V6 going lean on full throttle, use colder sparkplugs. A change from Autolite AG-42 to AG-32 was suggested. Replacing the distributor's secondary spring with a lighter equivalent allowed more vacuum advance. A slightly bigger primary jet, and relatively bigger secondary jet for the two-barrel Holley Weber carb, cured leaning out.

The modifications brought improved throttle response, a one mpg improvement in fuel economy, and a measurable power gain. Stock maximum rear wheel horsepower was 64 units at four grand; it was now 76 horses at 4500rpm. Geraghty Dyno-Tuned Products of Glendale California was working on a boxed kit of the abovementioned V6 mods. There were two downsides: first, tight engine compartment access made the job tricky. The distributor was buried against the firewall, and the passenger side extreme rear sparkplug was a bear to get to as well.

Consumer Reports found the same sparkplug access problem on the Mustang II V8. This case involved loosening an engine mount to change the sparkplug! The second issue with any modification was emissions. There were doubts an engine could pass the smog test with performance mods, at least in California.

The same applied to bolt-on turbo kits. Found on a variety of '70s vehicles from Vega Wagons to Datsun Zs, they reduced hydrocarbons and nitrogen oxides, but tended to raise carbon monoxide. Still, they brought welcome gains when performance was waning, and there was a kit for Mustang II and Capri V6s.

Spearco Mustang II V6 Turbo

Spearco Performance Products, run by George Spears, added a Rajay turbo to the V6/four-speed power team with impressive results. As per other bolt-ons of the era, the cylinder head stayed in place, so the stock compression ratio remained, promising a pure gain with the extra 10psi of peak boost. In the tight environs of the Mustang II engine bay, George Spears said an experienced mechanic with tools meant for tight spaces would take ten hours for the turbo installation. The kit was designed for minimum disruption. Normal pollution controls remained; so too factory a/c, power steering and power brakes.

There was no turbo wastegate or pop-off valve. The dual exhaust system was arranged so that removing stock mufflers and using two resonators would produce enough back pressure to limit turbo boost to 10psi. Even so, Spear's R&D brought further mods to ward off detonation. Primaries had their carb jet sizes increased from 0.056 to 0.0605in. Secondaries were larger, too, from 0.071 to 0.073in. Ignition timing was still ten degrees BTDC, but the kit needed colder sparkplugs and the best gas around. This was a challenge in the Golden State, where Hi Test was a precious commodity.

The Mustang II Mach I continued the famous Mach I name through 1974-78, devoid of the spoilers of Mustang II's other sport packs. A '78 Mach I V8 is shown. (Courtesy Mr Concourse)

The Mustang II Mach I, was an upscale sports/luxo package for the fastback bodystyle. With standard V6 and other goodies, it was a standalone pack forerunner of the '78 King Cobra. (Courtesy Mr Concourse)

Spearco research led to Champion sparkplugs (N59G Gold Palladium) gapped at 0.028in, and combined with a Delta Mark X capacitive discharge ignition system. The sparkplugs and Delta Mark X were not included in the $625 kit. The results were impressive though. At 9.4 seconds for 0-60mph and 17.5 seconds at 83.5mph in the ¼ mile, the Spearco-blown Mustang II V6 was two seconds faster in the ¼ mile than a stock V6. It was even one half-second swifter than 1974's Capri 2800.

In spite of the accommodative engineering, the finished package had to be approved by the California Air Resources Board (CARB). There was still plenty of speed equipment available from the aftermarket, but for the track, strip and hillclimb, not public roads. The enthusiast and internal combustion engine had come up against their stiffest opposition yet. It was from the lobby groups, legislators and the laws they wrought. Collectively, they made the privately owned automobile public enemy number one.

Many senators were critics of the auto industry, and what they felt was its slow progress to clean and efficient engines. The 1970 385 series 370 horse Ram Air 429 V8 was quite efficient. Tick the Drag Pack order blank, and an 11.3:1 comp ratio added five wild horses. However, somehow senators like California's George Brown thought that it was more efficient to drive a low compression smogger that ran hotter and thirstier than its predecessors, relative to power output.

The 1970 Muskie Smog Bill spelt the end of the traditional high output V8 with sharp throttle response, all aided by a high compression ratio and leaded high test gas. Whatever the true extent of the various senators' personal beliefs, they were influenced by environmental activists and lobby groups. Such groups had a puritanical zeal, heretofore never seen in North American history. In February 1974, *Motor Trend*'s John Christy used the description "fuel-abusing ecological extremism."

Such activism was forced as a counterpoint to the dominance of the Big 3 automakers during the postwar era. Corporations that bought up bus companies in '50s California, only to close them down and promote private car

Above left: This '78 Mach I's 2bbl 302 V8 was the same unit one found in the King Cobra. It could also be optioned in Mustang II Ghia. Either way, all roads led to 139bhp and 250lb/ft. (Courtesy Mr Concourse)

Above right: Personalizing a Mustang is traditional. The Cobra II package allowed one to do just that, for $312 in 1976 MY. (Courtesy Bryan Tyner www.kcclassicauto.com)

ownership. More extreme elements in the environmental group wanted walking, the bicycle and public transport. Only a ban on private car usage in inner city areas would placate them. In the meantime CARB was attempting to force the retrofitment of nitrogen oxide pollution control equipment on 1966-70 passenger cars. The penalty for non-compliance was the withholding of 1976 licenses.

The few remaining speed shops like Randall American, DKM and Spearco tried to stay legal. They moved to new 'complete' performance packages. These blended more punch with plush, plus handling and visual delights. The DKM Macho Trans Am and Spearco Mustang II Turbo were examples. The latter had a $378 handling package and aero/racing addendum. A 1in front sway bar and ⅞in rear baseball bat helped keep things on the level. There were lowering springs, with the front replacements being much stiffer than stock.

Four Koni shocks rounded out the package, and *Road & Track* measured the lateral skidpad improvement. Respective readings for stock V6, Spearco Turbo and Capri 2800 were 0.683g, 0.714g, and 0.726g. Slalom speeds were along similar lines of progress at 51.7mph, 54.2mph and 54.9mph respectively. So the chassis upgrades nearly put Mustang II on par with the lighter Capri. The only onion in the ointment was Mustang II's limited

suspension travel, like other sporty domestics. The lowering job increased the chance of bottoming out.

Stick to glass-smooth roads or less bumpy tracks and the Spearco Turbo handled like a dream. It also cut a dashing figure. Spearco-designed front and rear spoilers on the outside and 13in padded steering wheel on the inside made one feel special. The enthusiast was no longer a teenybopper driving a hot V8 in primered shell.

The Spearco Turbo, and other low volume packages, provided the complete sports/luxo personal car that buyers wanted. However, by 1974 this was a very small buyer group. Most of the nearly 400,000 were satisfied with a normal Mustang II. As Jim Brokaw wrote in *Motor Trend*, the standard four-cylinder Mustang II notchback, with $110 radial tire option, was a $2995 bargain. Punchier than earlier 2-liter emissionized Pintos, with a ride/handling and performance/economy blend Vega would struggle to match. Ghia had all this, plus new style American luxury for $3346. Brokaw even opined that the $3539 Mach I V6 would fuel dreams of Riverside and the Nürburgring. That last thought would have pleased Henry Ford II, but was probably a bit of a stretch. However, all except *Consumer Reports* agreed that Mustang II was a pleasant car, but was that enough?

On the 7th day Big Lee decreed there would be a V8 …

There were two curious things about the UK market 1975 Mustang II Ghia V8. For one, it had right-hand drive steering – this being available in the UK from May 1975. It was a relatively crude conversion, directed by UK agent Ford Personal Import Export. It relied on chain drive to allow steering on the right. The second curiosity was the 58.1/41.9% front-to-rear weight distribution. With a/c fitted, this became 59.9/40.1%. It was commensurate with a big-block first gen Stang, but made *Autocar* magazine question if Mustang II had been planned with V8 power in mind.

Mustang II had been planned with V8 punch. In fact, Mustang has never been available without V8 power if one lived south of the border, down Mexico way. In Mexico, a V8 motorvated Mustang II was a necessity. Ford's factory near Mexico City didn't make the 2.3 Lima I4, or 2.8 Cologne V6. In this market the available Fords represented low volume, high quality production for affluent Mexican customers. Private car ownership not being as prevalent as in America, Mexican production focused on just Maverick, Mustang II, Galaxie and F100/F350/F600 truck lines. In this era Mexican production was for Mexico. Like other South American countries, local production with high local content was the only way to get around prohibitive import duties. It was back in 1962 that the Mexican government set out the requirements for a viable car manufacturing industry. Limits on production, model ranges and a minimum of 60% local content were abided by Ford and others. It set up some detail differences between Mexican Fords and their US counterparts.

There was no Pinto economy subcompact for Mexico, and Mexican Mustang IIs had less stringent impact bumpers, plus pollution dictates in line with 1972 US smog law. Naturally, cars made here wouldn't be sold in America.

However, there were many similarities between the 1974 Mustang II 302 V8 and its eventual 1975 North American counterpart. Getting the 302 V8 to fit the Pinto-based Mustang II was the job of Ford USA man Jack Mohr and his Mexican design staff. A neat touch to be seen on all Mustang II V8s was a heavy plastic duct carrying air from behind the right headlamp around the 12-volt battery, thereby cooling it, into the side of the air cleaner housing.

Several were the mods necessary to permit the V8 conversion. It would have been hard to imagine a home

Top: You could have the Rallye Package on Mustang II Ghia. One could also combine the Cobra II pack with the base 2.3 Lima motor, to challenge Toyota Celica. (Courtesy Bryan Tyner www.kcclassicauto.com)

Bottom: Four on the floor was standard on Mustang II. Here, the German four-speed Hummer, was a light shifting companion for the gas-sipping Lima motor. (Courtesy Bryan Tyner www.kcclassicauto.com)

mechanic matching the refined and measured approach of Ford's engineers. The radiator yoke was moved forward. A new support shifted the radiator 3in forward too. The '75 MY grille was moved forward to the sheetmetal edge, and sported a larger eggcrate pattern. The hood was lengthened to match, and raised one ½in. The engineers were going for greater cooling space. The 302 V8 cars had an upgraded radiator core, 90 degree oil filter mount, and a smaller alternator.

It was a real custom job, with different radiator supports, cowl top panel, front side inner and outer stampings, unique dash panel, special reinforced front floor and transmission tunnel stampings. The rear part of the floor was reinforced, and the steering column was moved to the right compared to V6 cars. The V8 itself sat 1.5in rightwards to clear the steering column. The side rails of the second crossmember were strengthened, and heavier gage steel was used for front suspension spindles, lower control arms and compression struts.

The father of the modern assembly line process, Henry could see the convenience and economies of scale achieved by applying all of the above structural and material upgrades to all 1975 Mustang IIs. So come 1975, four-cylinder and V6 Mustang II owners could also enjoy the improved hardware. V8 cars also got better suspension, tires and brakes. Front spring rates rose from the V6 a/c spec 350lb/in to 375lb/in, which was the same upgrade as the Mustang II Competition Suspension option. Rear spring rates increased from 101 to 106lb/in. The Department of Transportation (DOT) tire load rules also necessitated upgrading from the Mach I V6's BR70-13s to CR70-13s.

The Windsor V8 weighed 213lb more than the Cologne V6. To compensate for a possible increased thirst, Dearborn's designers made an auxiliary 3.5 gallon gas tank optional. Placed in the rear ¼ panel, it boosted tank capacity to 16.5 gallons. However, real world fuel economy made the unstrained V8, nearly as frugal as the V6.

One of several variations between the Mexican and US Mustang II V8s concerned flywheel size. The Mexican cars had a different floorpan and 11in flywheel, the US cars had a small 10in flywheel. Space was tight on Mustang II concerning bellhousing to subframe space. The limited space is determined by flywheel size, and affects what exhaust manifold or header system can be employed.

Below: In the '70s a brushed metal-effect dash spelled high performance. Made popular by the Trans Am, it was quickly adopted by all speedy domestics. (Courtesy Bryan Tyner www.kcclassicauto.com)

Unlike the '80s street sleeper look, the '70s sporty car scene was all about flaunting one's appearance. The public couldn't get enough of appearance packages like Cobra II. (Courtesy Bryan Tyner www.kcclassicauto.com)

According to *Road & Track,* a better trimmed trunk than the Mercedes W108 S class. With the rear seats folded, trunk capacity was 18ft³. (Courtesy Bryan Tyner www.kcclassicauto.com)

Flywheel size is believed to be one reason why 1975 US Mustang II V8s were automatic only, whereas those south of the border could get a four-speed. Another reason was certification cost, for getting the Mustang II V8 smog passed in America. To get it to pass the EPA's 50,000 mile test, costs doubled for doing auto and stick shift 302s. In addition, US smog law got much stricter for 1975. It's very difficult to drive a stick shift V8 car steadily enough for the test, especially concerning hydrocarbons.

More and more folks liked the convenience of automatic drive, and so ticked that option box. With few potential four-speed buyers, FoMoCo decided not to risk a four-speed car with poor driveability, but a four-speed would return. In the meantime, a Ford C4 three-speed automatic and 3.00:1 rear axle would suffice. This would prove to be the only choice for California and high altitude-bound Mustang II V8s. It was so for the Mustang II's entire run. In Mexico, laxer smog laws and gross ratings spelt 205 horses at 4600rpm and 295lb/ft at 2600rpm. All using an 8.2:1 CR and Ford GPD two-barrel carb.

In America, the strict '75 smog standards and net ratings brought 129bhp at four grand, and 213lb/ft at 1800rpm. Compression ratio was only 8:1, so the 302 V8 could supp regular gas in 49 state form. Californian V8 Mustang IIs used dual catalytic converters to meet the Golden State's even stricter laws. Dual cats promised better throttle response because they allowed more advanced ignition timing. However, the price of such civic mindedness was a drop to 122 horses. All '75 MY Ford engines were using EGR to some degree: more so in California and high altitude areas.

Ford took a dual exhaust, dual cat approach to V8 emissions. Chevrolet was using dual cats on its Nova cop issue cars, and wanted to do the same on mainstream cars like Monza, and the pending '77 Camaro Z/28. However, the bean counters restricted Chevrolet to a single cat and resonators. Dual cats, as used by FoMoCo, were considered a luxury. For Mustang II Mach I V6 and all V8 cars, it was a dual system: headers leading to a muffler for each bank of the V8, then into one big resonator located on the right passenger side.

It would seem that Ford had the edge in this Ford versus Chevy rivalry. However, in this era 49 state buyers were relieved they didn't need a cat. At this time catalytic converters weren't looked at too fondly. They tied one to using more expensive unleaded gas which, due to a lack of refinery capacity and other shenanigans, wasn't that easy to find. Two-way catalytic converters would expire prematurely and expensively. They were very reliant on how an engine was tuned. It was harder to keep the air/fuel mix at the optimal stoichiometric ratio, without fuel-injection. Burnt out cats were annoying and expensive.

Optioning to the heart's content

In any case, between 1975 and 1982, 302 V8 fans were restricted to a Motorcraft two-barrel carb. Only the big-block 460 V8 had a four-barrel carb in 1975 and 1976. For all Mustang II V8 buyers up to spring 1976, it was the 2bbl 302 and C4 autobox with three-speed ratios of 2.46/1.46/1.00, plus aforementioned 3.00 rear axle. However, beyond this one could still build a Mustang as desired. As mentioned by

Lee Iacocca requested both notchback and fastback bodystyles, as part of Mustang II's plan. The classic Shelby look of Cobra II got one noticed. (Courtesy Angie)

Car and Driver in its 1978 Buyer's Guide, it was wise to arm yourself with several pencils, to deal with all those order blanks!

The Ghia notchback was desired by many. It was the default choice small luxury car. Jumping from a 1974 $2895 to $3346, brought enough finery to produce a mini Lincoln. There was a full vinyl roof and side protector strip, front fender pinstripes and a $96 luxo interior. That luxury meant passenger-side digital clock, crushed velour upholstery and faux walnut woodgrain dash inlays. Said walnut burl continued onto the door cards. All this went with standard four-speed Hummer box and Lima 2.3 I4, although the $229 V6 was a practical option.

Radials were only $33 on Ghia. Across the base/Ghia/Mach I range, automatic/air con/bumper guards cost a respective $204/$368/$36. A leatherette-rimmed steering wheel was $29 and sunroof $143. As per domestic car practice, Mustang II grouped desirable and popular related options into a single package. The Anti-Theft Group included Ford's Anti-Theft alarm system. First seen on 1973 full-size Fords, the system sounded the Mustang II's horn for 5 minutes, if a nefarious character opened a door or luggage compartment, when armed. Other 'Security Protection' package inclusions were interior hood release, a lock on the spare tire, front floor mats, door edge guards and lockable gas cap.

However, true security was afforded by the Competition Suspension option. As with big brother Gran Torino and American Express, never leave home without it. A larger 0.815in swaybar replaced the standard stock bar. A 0.75in rear swaybar arrived, where there had been none before. Spring rates climbed from 350lb/in front and 101lb/in rear, to 375lb/in and 123lb/in front and rear respectively. To achieve the stiffer rear spring rate, an extra leaf was added to the rear suspension. The front spring

eye was now solid, not voided. Very importantly, three-position Gabriel Strider shocks were included.

Gabriel Striders sounded good. *Road & Track* did a performance shock test in 1975, using a '74 Vette, and Gabriel Striders tested out best, outperforming pricier Koni and Bilstein. They came factory set on the softest setting with Mustang II. However, they worked best on full hard. This was the assessment of *Road & Track*'s engineering editor, when he tried a new Mustang II V8 at the Dearborn test track, for the September 1974 issue. In the November '74 issue of *Road Test*, the Competition Suspension was a winner. On a Mach I V8, it went 5mph faster around the 150ft Dearborn skidpad. The Mustang II 302 with Competition Suspension could also corner 8-10mph faster!

The sentiment was that whatever harshness the sports suspension brought was more than compensated for by

better car control. There was more traction too, less nosedive kept the rear tires planted to get the power down. It also reduced front end float. All this hardware was best utilized with the 302 V8, but could be applied to Lima 2.3 and Cologne V6 powered cars as well. The Competition Suspension was included in the Rallye Package. This pack cost a reasonable $133 in 1974, and brought many useful items under one roof. Added items included HD cooling system,

The '77 MY availability of a black and gold get-up for Cobra II, predated the movie release of *Smokey & The Bandit*. However, there was some influence from similar Trans Ams. (Courtesy Parker Productions www.facebook.com/ Parker ProductionsPhotography)

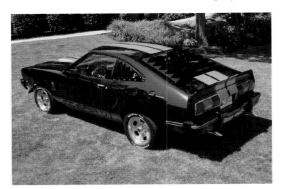

By 1977, the Cobra II package retailed for a not inconsiderable $514, but its popularity continued unabated. (Courtesy Mike Baker)

steel-belted radials, digital clock, limited-slip differential, remote control side mirrors and leatherette-wrapped steering wheel.

The top 195/70-13 radial tire was a separate option. Such 'mix & match' optioning was part of the fun. You could get the Rallye Package on Ghia notchback, and come 1975 the Ghia got even more opulent. It went to a half-padded vinyl roof with opera windows. The latter being practically mandatory for any '70s luxo cruiser. In 1975, the Silver Luxury Group turned that half-vinyl roof silver, and the crushed velour interior cranberry. By 1977 it was disco fever and package fever. Mustang II plainly brought more choice than that black-only Model T could have dreamt of.

Covering all bases, there was now a Sports Appearance Group for '77 Ghia, color-keyed to black or tan exterior paint jobs. One could add an Appearance Décor Group to base hardtop and midspec 2+2 hatchback.

By the late '70s cars like Cobra II became suburban status symbols, as much as they were also reminders of past muscle car glory. (Courtesy www.hooters.com)

The former made the luxurious sporty, and the latter turned the plain into luxurious. Unfortunately, Mustang II, like most domestic sporty cars, didn't have a reclining seat option. However, for '77 MY there was a four-way manually adjustable driver's seat. Adjustments concerned fore and aft, plus height.

Mustang's Fashion Accessory Group was designed with lady buyers in mind. Included in the package were Fresno cloth trim and the security aid of a lighted interior the moment one of the door handles was raised. It also seemed that good gas mileage came standard. To match Pinto, a mid '75 MY MPG spec was introduced on Californian Mustang II 2.3s. This involved a catalytic converter and taller 3.18 rear axle versus the former 3.55:1. Post Energy Crisis One, this garnered nice 23mpg city/34mpg highway EPA numbers.

For 1976, the MPG spec became standard for all four-cylinder Mustang IIs. The German Hummer four-speed was

a nice, light shifting aid to gas mileage. However, compared to imports, Mustang II and other domestics didn't put pedals on the same plane, which was awkward. The engineers were getting to grips with tightening emissions. Oh to be a race car engineer. With few limitations Ford Europe put 220bhp 2-liter Pinto I4s into rear drive rally Escorts. In the European Touring Car Championship (ETCC) the 1974 Ford Capri's Cologne V6, was a 3.4-liter 24-valve DOHC job that made 450 ponies. This wasn't on the options list!

The black and gold '77 Cobra II was mostly influenced by the 1966 Hertz Shelby GT 350s. These follow up rental Shelbys originated the exterior color scheme. (Courtesy Mike Baker)

Battling pollution & economy law

In 1975 North American EPA reality, the Lima 2.3 and Cologne V6 were down to 83 and 97 horses respectively. The feds were hoping for air as pure as that in the Swiss Alps. Dearborn fought back in 1976, raising the I4 and V6's respective outputs to 92 and 102bhp. Stricter pollution regs then dropped them down to 89 and 93 respective horses in 1977. They were re-rated yet again for 1978. The now 9:1 CR Lima 2.3 was back where it started, 88bhp at 4400rpm and 118lb/ft at 2800rpm.

The overall EPA number for a four-speed four-cylinder 1978 Mustang II was 26mpg, for the 49 state version. It was 24mpg for Californian and high altitude editions. This small car weighed 2712lb, rode on B78-13 bias belted rubber, and retailed for $3555. Certainly an economy car by 1978 standards, but what about 1985? Muscle cars meant nothing to President Carter, and 1978 saw the introduction of CAFE. The government-decreed good citizen approach directed automakers to have a fleet average of 18mpg in 1978, or else. Cars not meeting that target would receive a gas guzzler tax, and Uncle Sam would get an instant donation.

The fuel crisis saw oil imports make up a large part of America's import tab. To reduce reliance on Middle Eastern oil, the federal government decided to interfere with the purchasing decisions of consumers. Anyone that could afford to buy a V8-powered car that broke the 18mpg rule would be penalized for doing so. Under CAFE the plan was to step up the fleet average to 27 mpg, by 1985.

Below left: The Cobra II wasn't the ultimate factory Mustang II. That accolade belonged to the one-year-only 1978 King Cobra! (Courtesy Mark)

Below right: With its 4in bore and 3in stroke, the 302 was the only V8 used by Mustang II. FoMoCo's 302 V8 is one of the all-time great affordable high performance engines. (Courtesy Mark)

So eventually, even a 1978 four-cylinder Mustang II would become a gas guzzler, according to the EPA. Ford's next generation of small cars, and those from everyone else, would have to go front drive, and have several Weight Watchers sessions. It was in this post-apocalyptic, 0-50mph era that many feared the V8's demise. Fortunately, reports of its death were greatly exaggerated. It wasn't 1984 or 1985 yet. While Big Brother was making his plans, Ford was busy combining Mustang II with the 302 V8.

The '76 Mustang II Cobra II's size and color scheme harked back to the original Shelby GT350. Many wanted a return to smaller, sportier Mustang times. (Courtesy Shelby American Inc.)

want more
F.P.M.?*
try a Shelby GT

*That's Fun-Per-Mile—yours aplenty in these *two* great new GT cars from Shelby American.

There's more F.P.M. when you have reserve performance. The GT 350 carries a 306 horsepower 289 cubic inch V-8. The GT 500 is powered by the 428 cubic inch V-8, descended from the 1966 LeMans winning Ford GT.

The F.P.M. is higher when steering is competition-quick, suspension is firm. Driving's *fun* with the safety of an integral roll bar, shoulder harnesses, disc front and drum rear brakes, wide-path 4-ply nylon tires.

Driving's *fun* with the Shelby brand of comfort and style. For more F.P.M., see your Shelby dealer P.D.Q.

SHELBY G.T. *350 and 500* **The Road Cars** Powered by *Ford*

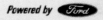

Shelby American, Inc., 6501 W. Imperial Highway, Los Angeles 90009

Mustang II & rivals

"New Mustang II combines value and economy while maintaining its sport heritage," that was the claim from Ford's PR machine for the '74 model year. There is some evidence to support their claim. Mustang II's stiffest and most direct test would come from traditional rival Chevrolet. The car in question was the Monza, and it followed closely in the Mustang II's tire tracks. Subtle differences did exist, as is typical of the Blue Oval vs Bow Tie rivalry. Based on the subcompact Vega, the Monza had an all-new body and more refined version of Vega's rear suspension. Like Pinto to Mustang II, the idea was less NVH with the larger, upscale cousin.

Monza had Vega's aluminum block I4, and was going to have GM's new rotary engine too. Inadequate durability meant the high transmission tunnel was the only legacy of rotary planning. Chevrolet instead inserted the small-block V8. It was a 262ci unit at first, with the 305 V8 to follow. By '77 MY the 305 V8 could have a four-speed. Considering the badge engineered 3.8 V6-powered Buick Skyhawk, GM set up Monza H-body to match Mustang II option for option, pound for pound, except in one area: quality.

It seemed that Monza was affected by the same poor build quality and unreliability that afflicted Vega. *Road & Track* in February 1975 described the Buick's build quality as "atrocious." More than that, there were signs of rushed engineering concerning brakes and suspension. Early GM H-bodies exhibited worrying braking performance during independent testing. Aside from very long stopping distances, *R&T*'s test Skyhawk had severe brake fade. So much heat was generated by the front disks that the plastic wheelcover mounting surfaces melted, causing said covers to fall off!

Right from the start Mustang II's disk/drum system was okay. *Motor Trend*'s Mach I V6 hauled down from 60mph in 133ft, in its December 1973 issue. This was only 5ft longer than *R&T*'s 1975 BMW 530i, which had four wheel disks and was over twice the price. In March '76 *Road Test* went one better, doing 20 laps in a Mustang II Cobra II V8. Admittedly after this exercise the brakes were toast, but they recovered after a 15 minute nap. From the earliest tests,

Sporty Mustang II: The Pony becomes a Cobra

By invoking the spirit of the classic '65 Shelby GT 350, the '76 Mustang II Cobra II fueled auto dreams at a time when such fantasies were rare. (Courtesy Bryan Tyner www.kcclassicauto.com)

Mustang II garnered comments about it being well made, plush and very quiet. It seems Henry was better prepared than the General.

Being the newest kid on the block, Monza was in the limelight. Snazzy styling and being 1975 *Motor Trend* Car of the Year helped. Ford diffused some of the Chevy's thunder, by having Mustang II 302 V8 ready for '75 MY. Even though '74 Mustang II sales were strong without a V8, it seems the coming of Monza V8 prompted Ford to spend money getting the 302/auto power team emissions certified sooner. Although auto-only in 1975, the 302-powered Mustang II had a clear edge in acceleration and handling versus the 262 cube Monza automatic. Both were tested by *Road & Track* in January 1975. It was 0-60mph in 10.5 seconds versus 13.4 seconds, for Ford and Chevy respectively.

Motor Trend's November 1974 Mustang II versus Monza report, confirmed the result. Zero to sixty in 9.6 not 12.6 seconds, favoring Ford when comparing the 302/auto with the 262ci/four-speed Chevy power team. Respective ¼ mile figures also went Henry's way, with 17.5 against 19 seconds. The Chevy 4.4-liter V8 and Skyhawk's 3.8-liter V6 were on a performance par with the Mustang II Mach I V6.

If dealing with the GM H-body was like shooting fish in a 2-barrel carb, Mustang II would find a more suitable whale-sized target in the Mercedes 450SL. *Road & Track*'s 0-60mph time for the freer emissions-tuned '74 450SL was 10.2 seconds. The Mercedes took 5ft longer to stop from 80mph, registered 7dBA more noise at 70mph, and was slightly worse on the skidpad at 0.7g versus 0.72g. The Mustang II 302's lateral cornering force reading equaled the sporty BMW 2002tii. All figures recorded by *R&T* at around the same time.

The Mustang II versus Monza contest highlighted another quality of the '70s and '80s. Ford seemed ready at an earlier stage. GM's new products seemed to take longer to arrive, and once they did they needed a few model years before appropriate power teams and quality control were in place.

With or without quality, GM projected Monza's first year total at 200,000. 1974 had seen the sales slide of Camaro Z/28, Plymouth Barracuda, Dodge Challenger and glacial sales of Super Duty Firebirds. These rides, along with AMC Javelin, would not return in 1975. It was predicted that cars of the Z/28 and Trans Am's ilk were on the way out. Although the regular Chevy Camaro and Pontiac Trans Am did appear for '75 MY, it seemed Detroit had smaller fish to

Below left: The Cobra II package was developed by BORT Inc. It was added to standard cars by Jim Wangers' Detroit-based company, Motortown Corp, during 1976. (Courtesy Bryan Tyner www.kcclassicauto.com)

Below right: The Mustang II Cobra II delivered the upscale sports/luxury nature that pony car buyers demanded in the '70s. (Courtesy Bryan Tyner www.kcclassicauto.com)

fry. Ford's open policy in 1975 was that Maverick and the newish luxo Granada compact were where the action lay.

While the big dinosaur sport compacts seemed on the verge of extinction, the small luxury car typified by Monza and Mustang II appeared in the ascendancy. In mid 1974, Joe Oldham made the observation that 4 grand VW Bugs and 4½ grand Pintos were scurrying around. He said the latter came in the form of Mustang IIs. It was a cynical statement, given the numerous engineering changes between the two Fords. Could one then call a Caddy Seville a 12 grand Nova? It wasn't possible to have a 4 grand Pinto V6 in '74 MY. In the fuel crisis times and market freefall of 1974, Mustang II had the sports/luxo subcompact domestic game to itself, but this didn't last.

1975 saw the Monza Town Coupe and 2+2 arrive to tempt prospects respectively from Mustang II Ghia and fastback. The larger GM F-body was also resurgent. In the early '70s, GM had considered canning both Camaro and Firebird. However, the Camaro LT did well in 1975, and the Z/28 was only on hiatus. Combined Formula and Trans Am sales were over 40,000 that year. It seemed like Mustang II had commercial company. As part of downsizing, many former intermediate buyers switched to GM F-body. With easing gas prices after the '74 crunch, some sized up to the sport compact GM F-body.

Greater GM competition and lower gas prices explain Mustang II's lower 1975 total of 186,548 units. In the face of this stiff GM opposition, including a rising Corvette, Mustang II flew Henry's checkered sporty flag at a consistent 175,000 units average during 1975-78. As a downsizing trailblazer, it predated Cadillac's Nova to international size Seville creation. Plus, AMC's Hornet to Concord transition. Reworking an existing platform for refinement and luxury. Indeed, in a Modified Mustangs & Fords retrospective article Jim Smart

observed: "These humble, little ponies weren't just a rebodied Pinto, but a refined version of the Pinto/Bobcat platform."

A 1976 Mustang II Cobra II was driven by Farrah Fawcett in the TV show *Charlie's Angels.* She played private investigator Jill Munroe. (Courtesy Bryan Tyner www.kcclassicauto.com)

Smart noted differences from Pinto's engineering. Dearborn's engineers nicknamed Mustang II's modified front subframe the 'toilet seat.' The Competition Suspension also showed a set-up unique to Mustang II. Revised suspension geometry also made Mustang II more fun to drive than its upsized predecessors, as judged by Smart and others. A mid '74 MY running change had brought more steering feel to Mustang II, and there were other refinements.

Mustang II's rack and pinion power steering geometry involved a slight toe out action, concerning the outside wheel when cornering. This created a slower off-center response, more akin to Big Car handling. There was also no toe change during the suspension's jounce action. This was intended to reduce highway driving wind wander. In many ways Mustang II was delivering more overall car than mid-'60s equivalents. Put to one side Shelby and Boss Mustangs. Compare Mustang II to a normal early Mustang 289 V8 and things seem brighter.

Ford V8 – still first on race day!

In August 1965 *CAR* magazine posed the question on its cover, "How Mighty Is The Mustang?" The question was answered by Henry Manney III, whose work was often seen in *Road & Track* in the '60s and '70s. Manney went to George Trainor of Ford International (Brussels) to borrow a '65 Mustang for a jaunt down to the Targa Florio. A 200 horse Mustang 289 four-speed hardtop was provided for this purpose. This stallion, unburdened by pollution controls and devoid of a/c, hit 60mph in 11 seconds and did a top speed of 108mph. Some axle hop was experienced.

Top: The useful product placement of Cobra II on *Charlie's Angels* helped this Mustang II package sell 23,367 examples in '76 MY! (Courtesy Bryan Tyner www.kcclassicauto.com)

Bottom: With sales of 1,107,718, Mustang II didn't take a backseat to anything! (Courtesy Bryan Tyner www.kcclassicauto.com)

Autocar magazine's 1975 April 19 issue showed a new Mustang Ghia V8 hardtop did 0-60mph in 10.1 seconds, with a best recorded top speed of 110mph. It managed a 17.5 second ¼ mile at 76mph. Not bad for an automatic-equipped 302 V8 car that could run on regular and meet the strict '75 federal pollution regs, albeit in 49 state form. It seemed like 1975's 129 net horses were more honest than 1965's 200 gross ponies. Mustang II was also on par with contemporary sporty icons. In its February 25 1978 issue, *Autocar* tried the automatic Olds 403 powered Pontiac Trans Am. They got 0-60mph in 9.4 seconds, the ¼ mile in 16.4 seconds at 80mph, and 118mph top speed.

The Ford 302 was getting stronger during 1975-78. In 1977 the DuraSpark electronic ignition eliminated points, and produced more spark when the voltage dropped during start-up. DuraSpark's arrival coincided with a compression ratio hike from 8.0 to 8.4:1, and smaller diameter intake passages to boost low end torque. It worked: from 1975's 129bhp at 4 grand and 213lb/ft at 1800rpm, the latest 302 2bbl made 129bhp at 3400rpm and 242lb/ft at 2 grand. More good progress for 1978 saw that trusty 302 recalibrated to 139bhp at 3600rpm, and a very useful 250lb/ft at 1600rpm.

Car's August 1978 issue put the 302 V8-powered four-speed Mustang II King Cobra on 16.59 seconds at 82.41mph for the ¼ mile, with estimated 120mph top speed. This made the 3300lb Mustang II 302 V8 lineball with the aforementioned 3800lb 6.6-liter Trans Am. Mr Bandit had more than Smokey on his tail! Mid-16s were all a Corvette 350 of the era could manage, assuming one could locate a magazine test car that wasn't a ringer!

The 302 and Mustang II handled the expensive imports very well too. The new Mustang II V8 came out the same '75 MY as the doubly pricey North American BMW 530i. Comparing autobox editions there was similar acceleration to be had, up to 80mph. *Road & Track*'s 0-80mph time for the 1972 Mercedes 280SEL 4.5 V8 was 19 seconds. *Autocar*'s equivalent time for the Mustang II Ghia V8 was 19.2 seconds. A tremendous feat, given 1975 pollution regs were a lot stricter. Using *Autocar* magazine's 0-60mph, ¼ mile and top speed data, this 1975 Ghia V8 was virtually identical to the looser smog controlled 1973 Mustang Grande automatic. Ford Mustang II versus Mustang One, it was 10.1/17.5/107mph against 10.4/17.7/108mph respectively.

Finding comparable cars in Europe was never easy in the '60s and '70s. The US and Euro markets were so different. For overall size and weight, the 1975 Ghia V8 approximated the BMW 528 automatic. Standing start acceleration was equal until over 80mph. From this point, pollution-control-free Euro cars won out. In Europe, where specialist importers handled American car supply, prices were high and sales volume was low. In the UK, the Mustang II Ghia was two thirds the price of a BMW 528, whereas in America it was half the price of the better-specified 530i. The times the Mustang lived in should also be considered. It was an era of blanket speed limits. When *Autocar* tried it '74 Ghia V6, both Britain and West Germany had temporary 50mph speed limits. America adopted a 55mph limit and kept it. All to save gas in the wake of OPEC's oil embargo.

The fact the Mustang II V8 could exceed 100mph was becoming academic. However, its European-style refinements had value for today's buyer. The Euro design bug was catching, and not only with strong Mercury Capri sales. The Capri accounted for around 120,000 units in 1973. Chevrolet's boss had been driving a Mercedes. Impressed by the Swabian's high-speed straightline tracking, Chevy engineers gave Monte Carlo lots of steering caster. Radials, disk brakes and the '73 Pontiac Grand Am even had a steering-column-mounted

headlight dimmer switch. Judging from GM's advertising, it looked like no one would be saying car hold anymore. These new-age cruisers all lived in garages!

Mustang II featured much of this new direction. It showed such philosophy worked better on a smaller car than a pre-downsized domestic intermediate. The Mustang II was an early domestic adopter of the radial tire. From the start the '74 Mach I came with BR70-13s as standard, and CR70-13s as an option. The latter was the standard tire on '75 Mustang II V8s, with 195/70 R13s optional. Goodyear was an early domestic maker of the radial tire, but the American tire industry as a whole was slow to the radial party. Even in 1974, 70 series 14 in radial performance tires were largely unavailable from the US tire industry. This left domestic buyers to select 70 series bias-belted covers. With Mustang II living in the 13in rim subcompact neighborhood, it was easier to get the ride and handling advantage of radials.

Mustang II placed wiper/washer controls on a column stalk, not the dashboard. The four-way driver-adjustable seat was a handy option. The Mercedes 450SL and Mustang II both had easy-to-use, single buckle three-point

In a 1976 TV commercial for Mustang II, a Cobra II was featured with the tagline 'Mustang II Boredom 0.' These were indeed interesting times. (Courtesy Bryan Tyner www.kcclassicauto.com)

inertia reel front seatbelts. This made Mustang II one of the few '74 MY cars for which buyers didn't have to fear the federally mandated Interlock seatbelt enforcer. The little Ford had one big advantage over the German sporty car and most imports: nice impact bumpers.

The imports weren't really designed for the federal 5mph impact bumpers. Compliance involved ad-hoc devices that resembled diving boards. In contrast, all Mustang IIs came with front and rear color-keyed covers over a steel bar, with a bright metal accent strip inlaid concerning the covers. The rear amber taillight lenses were a neat Euro touch. Normally, domestic cars, as directed by bean counters, had red lenses that just went dim on one side to indicate a turn. That was the form, but *Autocar*'s test of the '75 Ghia 302 showed it had some substance, to be autobahn-ready.

At the MIRA (Motor Industry Research Association) speed bowl, the Ghia V8 hit a wind-assisted 110mph. However, dealing with the banking made it prudent to slow things to a tad over 100mph. Otherwise the front end float brought by the soft springing and front end weight bias made things edgy. The car on test didn't have the optional Competition Suspension. The only other feature to let down the Mustang in high-speed European driving were the weak headlights. Another domestic design, money-saving trait.

Cobra II – a '70s Shelby?
The Mustang has always been more at home in the pony car corral than on the bahn cruising with Benzs and Bimmers. So the 1976 Cobra II package costing $312 was perfectly in the Mustang wheelhouse. Ford had wrestled Cobra

By 1977, Cobra II was available in black with gold stripes. Ford had now taken over Cobra II completion from Motortown Corporation. (Courtesy tiltedkilt.com)

usage from Carroll Shelby. The Texan racer may not have been too happy, but it provided a look that finally got Mustang II fastback noticed on the street. *Road Test* carried out a social test in March 1976. The Cobra II got so many more appreciative glances than the Bertone-penned Dino 308 GT4 the magazine tested the same year.

The conclusion was that Henry knew Joe Q Public so much better than 'ol Enzo. The testers were practically serenaded when they drove in to a Howard Johnson restaurant. Only the Fonz could have got such a reception in 1976 … maybe. The response wasn't unexpected. When you combine a Polar White exterior with hood, roof and tail double racing stripes, there can only be one reaction. Can you say Shelby GT350?! Mustang fans thought they had seen a ghost. A brand spanking new 1965 Shelby GT 350? At a glance, perhaps.

For your OPEC stagflated $312 one got Cobra II side decals, front fender snake, aforementioned over-the-top hood/roof/tail dual blue stripes, color matched bumpers and spoilers, plus the ubiquitous Californian-style racing side mirrors. C-pillar louvers proudly carried the Cobra snake decal. There was a forward-facing hoodscoop, plus Cobra snake badge on the front blackout grille.

It would seem a ready-to-strike Cobra outfangs a prancing horse any day of the week on Mainstreet USA.

A V8 wasn't standard equipment – what gives?! In these troubled times, Henry exercised the free market Mustang option approach. The Cobra II pack could be added to four-cylinder, V6 or V8 Mustang II fastbacks. It seemed the public liked having a choice. A fair number of the 23,367 1976 Cobra IIs, sported four-bangers and ye olde Euro V6. Rest easy, Jill Munroe chose her Cobra II with the V8 option, or was that Charlie? The Mustang in question was a company car of the Charles Townsend Detective Agency after all.

Cobra II came with styled steel 13 x 5.5in sport rims. They were a 96 buck delete option. Accept them over forged alloys, and one got to keep the loot. Not Jill Munroe though; the little lady liked the forged Lacy alloys. *Road Test* really dug the whole Karma situation of a reborn Shelby Mustang too. In their excitement they took on a real GT350 in a street race. Predictably, their Cobra II steed came off second best. It was high 14s versus high 17s in the playground of wishful thinking. In the real world of 1976, Mustang had to accept catalytic convertors, and a federally forced diet of unleaded gas. A now sober *Road Test* scribe said: "We look for Volkswagens to awe."

As part of the upgrade for V8 power, Cobra II 302s like this car have HD front brake pads and improved rear drum linings. The HD drums from the Pinto wagon were also employed. (Courtesy Mike Baker)

White exterior and dual red racing stripes were one of the expanded color combinations of the 1977 Cobra II package. The optional $173 Lacy forged spoke alloys were color matched. (Courtesy Christelynn Teed)

As a 49 state car, this 1977 Cobra II could and does have the four-speed stick shift. The Ford Europe-sourced, close ratio Type-E box has direct 1:1 top gear. (Courtesy Christelynn Teed)

Not a bad idea, using the Cobra II for pest control. The Volkswagen Sports Bug took 18 seconds for 0-60mph. *Road Test*'s Cobra II 302 automatic, only 9.9 seconds. Everything is relative; the only pity was that Herbie was busy racing the Mercedes 300D, and winning! A wise warrior carefully selects their opponent. Fairness would involve comparing two *Road & Track* tested Mustangs with four on the floor and 3.00 rear axle. From March 1967 a 225 horse 289ci notchback against an August '76 issue Cobra II with 134 net ponies. Respective 0-60mph and ¼ mile times for the two Mustangs were 9.7/17.4 seconds versus 10.4/17.7 seconds. Close, considering the younger car had smog gear, supped unleaded, and had power steering.

Racer Charlie Kemp tried on a '76 Cobra II for size at Laguna Seca. He lapped the track, including the famous Corkscrew, in 1 minute 39.31 seconds. The steering and handling were very predictable; handling was neutral. Negative points included the smogger 302 that wouldn't pull beyond 4500rpm, and under-damped front end that invited float. As a road car it did okay. The Kemp Cobra II racer lapped in 1 minute and 11 seconds!

Mustang II Cobra II was developed by BORT Inc, made up of Jack Purcell and Jack Juratovic. In 1976, Cobra IIs were part-built by Jim Wanger's company Motortown Corp, located in Dearborn, Michigan. Mustang II fastbacks were sent over to Motortown Corp, where the Cobra II package was fitted. Then it was on to the Ford dealers. It was common for the industry to outsource specialist work. However, Ford itself handled complete Cobra II production in 1977. That said, the new fastback T-top option, a Ford first, was designed and added by ASC (American Sunroof Corporation). Once again, Ford planned to bring T-top fitment in-house for '78 MY.

In February 1977, *Motor Trend*'s John Ethridge declared: "The convertible is dead. Long live the T-top!" With fears of federal rollover tests, there wasn't much choice. The public loved T-tops, and Ford's version was well designed and better built than most. The floorpan was braced up some, and the A-pillar/windshield area was also beefed up.

A single latch release, for the dual tint tempered glass panels, was easy and standard practice. Ditto the storage pouch in the trunk.

It was a case of more or larger repayments in 1977. The Cobra II pack now retailed for $514, T-tops were $750, Lacy-forged alloy rims cost $173 and the four-speed added $234. Finally four on da floor, for the 302 V8. The four-speed was a spring 1976 release. Not the old BW T10, but a Ford of Europe design. It could just about cope with Mustang II's 302, but not the '82 GT's 5.0. Ratios were 2.64 (1st), 1.89 (2nd), 1.34 (3rd) and direct 1 to 1 top. This Type-E single rail shifter was a stronger version of the European Type-3 four-speed.

The Type-E had a cast iron main case and alloy tail housing. Often nicknamed the 'Rocket' box, due to its association with the racing close-ratio four-speed, that itself was Type-E based. Indeed, *Autoweek* complained about the King Cobra's closely-spaced four-speed. It was a light and easy shifting box. In terms of

doortag numbers, an '82 Mustang GT 5.0's SROD Tremec box would have the number '4,' the Type-E carries a '5,' with Mustang II V6's BW four-speed denoted '6,' and the Hummer four-speeder on digit '7.'

Four-speeds were fun, and so was Cobra II's expanded color palate for 1977. In addition to white with blue stripes, one could have red stripes, green stripes, or go blue paint with white stripes and a black exterior with gold stripes. That black and gold combo was first released in California. It was a tribute to the black and gold 1966 Hertz Shelby GT350s that succeeded the rental firm's white with blue stripes GT350 of 1965. It could be said Cobra II was one of the first nostalgia, low volume retro muscle cars. Their ilk have proven lucrative Detroit business ever since.

Cobra II got a big visual makeover for '78 MY. Much would be in common with the pending King Cobra. The non-functional hoodscoop was now facing backwards, aero style. Interior door cards

The 302 V8 was a Mustang mainstay from 1968 to 1995. Here, in 302 2bbl form, it made 129bhp at 3400rpm on unleaded gas. (Courtesy Christelynn Teed)

no longer had metal trim. The over-hood/roof/tail color stripes had become a single broad band. The side Cobra II profile decal was now mid-⅓ placed, no longer lower body positioned. The single mid-color band was interrupted by a large, capital block letter Cobra script on the doors. The Roman numeral II was moved within the mid band, above the rear sidemarker lamp. This numeral was a golden yellow, a pinstripe in the same hue highlighted the outside of the profile mid-band, as well as the over the hood/roof/tail racing stripe. Said racing stripe now flowed fully over the impact bumpers. Such attention to exterior and interior trim detail would sadly die out in the '70s.

The American stallion
Just before Rocky Balboa became the Italian Stallion on the streets of Philly, Henry introduced not one, but three thoroughbreds for 1976 model year. Joining Cobra II were some Stallions.

This was a follow-up to the Sprint pack offered in 1972. The Sprint visual package was for Pinto, Maverick and Mustang, celebrating the summer games of the 1972 Munich Olympics. This time around Stallion was for Pinto, Maverick and Mustang II. There was a matte blackout front grille. Lower third middle, front and rear valence, window surrounds were all in black. A Stallion decal lived on the front fender, in place of Cobra II's snake. Inside it was full instrumentation, woodgrain finish dash and digital clock, like Ghia. Unlike Cobra II, Stallion could be a notchback. However, like Cobra II, Mustang II Stallion could enjoy I4, V6 or V8 motors.

Charlie's Angels Cobra II
In 1977 Burt Reynolds and the black and gold Trans Am became pop culture icons. However, a little earlier Farrah Fawcett and the Mustang II Cobra II were doing much the same thing on the small screen. It was all to do with Aaron Spelling's

In August 1976, *Car Craft*'s Bruce Caldwell said children would be happier in the back of a Cobra II than the 1965 Shelby GT350! (Courtesy Christelynn Teed)

internationally popular TV show *Charlie's Angels*. Between 1976 and 1981 viewers watched a trio of young ladies work for the Charles Townsend Detective Agency. Charlie Townsend was never seen, he communicated with his investigators, the Angels, via an office desktop speaker. Agency office manager John Bosley oversaw a smooth running operation. Charlie was played by John Forsythe, and Bosley by actor David Doyle.

To do their legwork the Angels needed wheels. This task fell to a fleet of Ford subcompacts. One 1976 Mustang II Cobra II, a tan Mustang II Ghia hardtop and an orange Ford Pinto hatchback. Spelling-Goldberg Productions were using the Ford Studio-TV Car Loan Program at the time, just like with concurrent show *Starsky & Hutch*. Married to actor Lee Majors at the time, Farrah Fawcett-Majors was a legend in her time. With a famous poster and much copied hairstyle, some of her glamor rubbed off onto Cobra II.

Being 1976, the Cobra II was only available in Polar White, which conveniently matched Mrs Fawcett-Major's very white teeth. To this day no one can decide which was brighter. The popular Cobra II's image certainly shone brightly. It was a '76 MY automatic car, with optional Lacy spoke alloy wheels and surprisingly, a small tow hitch! Well, the fairer sex are practical minded. This last item wasn't always visible. Interestingly, the rear Cobra II louvers carried no Cobra emblems, and the front grille Cobra badge was blacked out. Featuring the familiar Motortown Corp dashboard, side door card and shifter bezel brushed metal Cobra II decorations, the coupe had a medium blue vinyl interior.

Journalist Patrick Smith has recognised that two Cobra II cars were utilized during the show's 5 season run. Aside from the 1976 car described above, there was a second 1977 coupe used for the final season. Smith's reasoning is based on the fact that there were slight cosmetic changes done

through Cobra II's production life. With new actresses joining the cast virtually every season, new car interior and exterior shots with the new Angels had to be done. Continuity dictated that the same cars would have to be used.

With the above theory accepted, it seems the original '76 Cobra II V8 was featured in seasons 1 to 4. This car was subsequently bestowed to Jill Munroe's sister Kris, played by Cheryl Ladd, when she joined the Townsend agency. As occurred with the *Starsky & Hutch* Gran Torinos, continual stunt work took its toll. By the close of season 4, the '76 Cobra II V8 was looking rather worse for wear.

It is strongly believed that the original car suffered an expired V8 engine, and had to be replaced by another car for the

Top: Compared to its rival Chevy Monza, Mustang II Cobra II stayed faithful to the traditional pony car look. Unlike post 1978 models, it still resembled a Mustang. (Courtesy Christelynn Teed)

Bottom: For 1978 the Cobra II package was re-liveried. It had a new reverse hoodscoop, also shared with the coming King Cobra, also. (Courtesy Classic Auto Rides (NC))

5th season. This was the aforementioned second Cobra II, a sort of clone car it seems. It is suspected that the previous Cobra II was sold during the summer of 1979, to a mechanic that worked on the show's car. He apparently purchased the '76 Cobra II with blown engine, from his Ford dealer boss. The mechanic retained this coupe for many years in Whittier, California.

By 1979 the Mustang II was out of production. The new Foxstang had arrived, and was in evidence on *Charlie's Angels*. In the 4th season episode 'Toni's Boys,' an attempt was made on Kelly Garrett's life. Her Mustang II Ghia got blown up, and her rental car was a silver, gray Foxstang. By now the show was being supplied with Foxstangs, under the Ford Studio-TV Car Loan Program. However, continuity dictated another Cobra II would have to replace the original '76 Cobra II V8.

The Cobra II Kris Munroe drove in season 5, the replacement car, looked slightly different. The new car lacked a front fender V8 callout badge. It was also missing the Cobra II's rear ¼ window louvers. It seems the show got hold of a used 1977 Mustang II 2+2, and created a clone car. They dressed it up with Motortown Corp Cobra II items, to make it resemble the season 1 to 4 Cobra II.

Concerning the present whereabouts of the Charlie's Angels Mustang IIs, only info on the Farrah Fawcett Cobra II is known. The aforementioned mechanic sold the car in recent years, and its new owner started restoration work. The season 5 Cobra II clone car was believed to have been repainted blue, and wrecked in a stunt on a subsequent Aaron Spelling TV show. What happened to Kelly Garrett's Ghia hardtop is unknown. Usually, as occurred with the *Starsky & Hutch* Gran Torinos, the cars are sold off when a TV show concludes. The Garrett Ghia hardtop was driven by Jaclyn Smith during *Charlie's Angels'* entire 5 season run.

Kemp Cobra II

The memory of Parnelli Jones in a Mustang Boss 302, triumphing over Mark Donohue's Javelin in 1970 at the height of the SCCA's Trans Am series, was golden. However, pony cars, road circuit racing and the whole domestic performance scene quietly deflated thereafter. Automakers aren't so willing to put cash into a series with limited showroom sales return. With mainstream domestic buyers moving towards luxury groups, gas mileage packs, and away from sports models, the Big Three jumped ship.

The Kemp Cobra II was Charlie Kemp's privateer entry in the 1970s IMSA All-American GT category. The car was based on the Mustang II Cobra II. (Courtesy Dan Vaughan www.conceptcarz.com)

Set well back in the spaceframe chassis, the well-placed 351 Cleveland V8 contributed to a 46/54% weight distribution. The motor eventually made over 600bhp! (Courtesy Dan Vaughan www.conceptcarz.com)

IMSA had a couple of ideas to deal with the situation. The B F Goodrich Radial Challenge for grocery getters, and the Camel GT for the out and out racer crowd. Early on the latter was a happy hunting ground for Corvette, then predictably the imports came. BMW and Porsche, with an eye to boosting sales in the North American market, brought over their racers from the European Touring Car Championship (ETCC). To keep Bruce Greenwood's Vette company, IMSA had another idea. It was the 1975 All-American GT category.

This sub category was for the domestics, but the cars competed in the same races as the BMWs, Corvettes and Porsches. More than that, they were eventual outright race winners. Mike Keyser in the Chevy Monza, was an early flag waver for the U.S.A. Keyser and Al Holbert worked through the Monza's early reliability gremlins. Holbert and Keyser finished 1st and 2nd at Atlanta, and 1st and 3rd at Laguna Seca respectively. The Monza soon became a sought after sports car/sports sedan

category racer internationally. Former Trans Am series campaigner Horst Kwech (DeKon Engineering) started building Monza racers. One even went to Canadian racer Alan Moffat in Australia.

It should be noted the new All-American GT category racers went further from their production car cousins than even BMW, Corvette and Porsche. In the case of the Kwech built Monza, Moffat said the 600bhp fuel injected Chevy 350-powered car was like going to the moon! One couldn't buy a Monza with eight piston calipers or four wheel disk brakes, but IMSA did set some limits. The aim was to encourage the design, construction and competition of racers made from volume produced American parts. To this effect, the basic suspension layout of the production car had to be kept. From this point mods were free. The body had to retain the stock roof, windshield, door pillars and the top of the instrument panel.

The question was, where was Ford? There seemed to be an arms length, or no involvement from domestic automakers. It was GM policy that racing was off limits, for any of its divisions. Similarly, a local Blue Oval hero came from left field. The hero was Charlie Kemp with his Kemp Cobra II. It wasn't called a Ford, because FoMoCo wasn't helping, but it was a Monza track rival. Charlie Kemp set the basic parameters and then Bob Riley designed the car.

Kemp Cobra II was innovative – it was one of the first road race cars to use a custom tube spaceframe. To start with, Riley got the blueprints for the Mustang II's body. The inner panels were not employed, just the basic outer shell and the custom spaceframe. The floorpan was stressed, being epoxied and riveted to the outer shell. The stock Mustang II has a very upright front grille. To overcome this aero brickwall, Kemp said the design team made the front fascia like a watermelon!

On road and track, the Mustang II and Monza were rivals. The Kemp Cobra II challenged the less powerful Chevy Monza of Mike Keyser. It was classic Chevy versus Ford Trans Am racing! (Courtesy Nathan Petroelje www.roadandtrack.com)

So Kemp Cobra II ended up with a low, narrow body and rounded visage for optimal aero. The suspension stayed basically faithful to Mustang II's front unequal length A arms and rear live axle. Like the road car's optional Competition Suspension there were adjustable Gabriel shocks and swaybars. A Watts linkage tamed the live axle. Before this came a Ford NASCAR road racing 4-speed, and Frankland NASCAR rear end. Steering was by Mustang II's power steering rack and pinion set up, sans the actual power assist. Monza went the same Ford steering hardware route, since the set up was tough, and needed few racing mods. Only 3.3 turns lock to lock were required.

BBS alloys sized 15 x 12in front and 17 x 15in rear housed NASCAR four-wheel disk brakes. There were 12.2in vented rotors at all four corners. State of the art Goodyear Blue Streak racing tires were sized 25 x 10-15in front, and 25 x 13-15in rearwards. Naturally, the whole deal sat much lower than stock. The Schiefer clutch and aluminum flywheel of the cast iron 4-speed, had to deal with a Gapp & Roush 351 Cleveland V8. The race recipe ran to a steel crank, 4-bolt mains, Mister Rod conrods, custom 12.5:1 pistons, General Kinetics cam, and Gapp & Roush ported heads with titanium valves, springs and retainers. Using Kinsler mechanical racing fuel-injection and 102 octane gas, it made 570 horses at 7 grand and 530lb/ft at 4600rpm.

Road & Track's performance figures with 3.50 rear axle were 0-60mph in 4.1 seconds, 12.1 seconds ¼ mile at 126.5mph and 153mph top speed. With the right gearing these All-American GT category cars had the power and aero to top 200 mph! Handling was aided by setting the motor almost as far back as biblical times. The result was a very un-Mustang II-like 46/54 per cent front to rear weight distribution. This Mustang could pull over 1.2g on the skidpad. If only Charlie Kemp could show such fine engineering. The IMSA governing body wasn't that welcoming to Mr. Kemp's

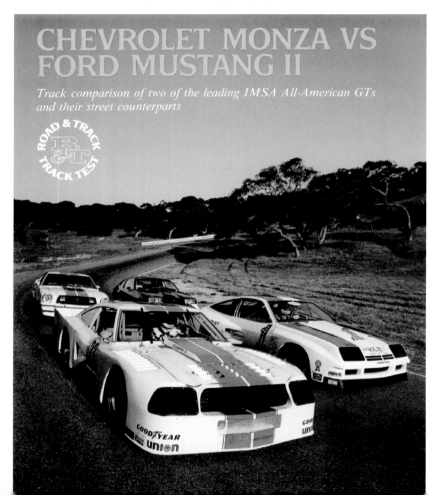

CHEVROLET MONZA VS FORD MUSTANG II

Track comparison of two of the leading IMSA All-American GTs and their street counterparts

ROAD & TRACK
TRACK TEST

wood's Corvette.

What about noise? Both are equally loud and we'd suggest ear plugs for anyone who gets within 10 ft of either car.

Both the swoopy Monza and the knee-high Cobra II represent the current state of the art in GT race car design. With crowd pleasing cars such as these tearing up the road courses of the U.S. and Canada we wouldn't be a bit surprised to see an American car win IMSA's 1976 Camel GT Challenge series.

IMSA racers had to retain the basic production car chassis layout, but mods were many. Roadgoing Mustang IIs, had access to a Total Performance 351C/W conversion kit. (Courtesy Nathan Petroelje www. roadandtrack.com)

Fuel-injected 351 Ford is well back in car's chassis.

Stark interior of the Cobra II leaves nothing hidden.

Cobra II front suspension is standard race car fare.

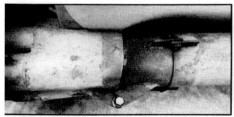

Exhaust pipe swings away as door is opened on Cobra II.

SPECIFICATIONS COMPARISON
Production & Racing Ford Mustang IIs

	Production	Racing
Price	$3992	$37,000
General:		
Weight, lb	3160 (curb)	2680 (race)
Weight distribution (with driver), front/rear,%	58/42	46/54
Wheelbase, in.	96.2	96.8
Track, front/rear	55.6/55.8	58.0/58.0
Length	175.0	171.0
Width	70.2	74.5
Height	49.7	43.0
Ground clearance	5.0	2.9
Usable trunk space	5.1 + 7.6	nil
Fuel capacity, U.S. gal.	13.0	31.7
Engine:		
Bore x stroke, mm	101.6 x 76.2	101.6 x 88.9
Displacement, cc/cu in.	4950/302	5753/351
Compression ratio	8.0:1	12.5:1
Bhp @ rpm, net	134 @ 3600	570 @ 7000
Torque @ rpm, lb-ft	247 @ 1800	530 @ 4600
Carburetion/fuel injection	one Motorcraft (2V)	Kemp Cobra II injection
Fuel requirement	unleaded, 91-oct	premium, 102-oct
Drivetrain:		
Gear ratios:		
4th	1.00	1.00
3rd	1.34	1.29
2nd	1.89	1.69
1st	2.64	2.32
Final drive ratio	3.00:1	3.50:1
Chassis:		
Brake system	9.3-in. discs front, 9.0 x 1.8-in. drums rear; vacuum assisted	12.2-in. vented discs front and rear
Swept area, sq in.	244	459
Wheels	cast alloy, 13 x 5½JJ	BBS alloy; 12 x 15 front, 17 x 15 rear
Steering type	rack & pinion, power assisted	rack & pinion
Tires	Firestone Steel Radial 500, 195/70R-13	Goodyear Blue Streak; 25.0 x 10.0-15 front, 25.0 x 13.0-15 rear
Front suspension	unequal-length A-arms, coil springs, Gabriel adjustable tube shocks, anti-roll bar	unequal-length A-arms, coil springs, Gabriel adjustable tube shocks, adjustable anti-roll bar
Rear suspension	live axle on leaf springs, Gabriel adjustable tube shocks, anti-roll bar	live axle on upper & lower parallel trailing arms and Watt linkage; coil springs, Gabriel adjustable tube shocks, adjustable anti-roll bar
Instrumentation:		
Instruments	120-mph speedo, 6000-rpm tach, 99,999.9 odometer, coolant temp, ammeter, fuel level	10,000-rpm tach, oil press., oil temp, coolant temp, transmission temp, rearend temp, voltmeter, fuel level
Warning lights	oil press., brake system, door ajar, headlights on, seatbelts, hazard, high beam, directionals	low fuel
Accommodation:		
Seating capacity, persons	4	1
Seat width, front/rear, in.	2 x 19.0/2 x 17.0	14.5
Head room, front/rear	36.0/33.5	37.0
Calculated data:		
Lb/bhp (test weight)	26.2	5.2
Mph/1000 rpm (4th gear)	23.1	21.0
Engine revs/mi (60 mph)	2600	2850
Piston travel, ft/mi.	1300	1665
Brake swept area, sq in./ton	139	310

privateer status. Until the officials were happy, Kemp was restricted to the Le Mans GTX category.

It wasn't until the 6th race of the 1976 season, that the Kemp Cobra II could make its IMSA debut. It was certainly fast, reaching 212mph at Daytona. Unfortunately, Charlie Kemp's problems didn't end once he was allowed to join the series. One of the reliability issues was engine durability. The original 351C lacked block strength. It couldn't handle the high output, and block-side blowouts occurred. The Mike

Keyser Monza's Weber carb 350 V8, was well down on power and torque. Nearly 35 horses shy, and 90lb/ft was amiss versus the potent 351C.

Kemp switched to an Australian-built 351C, as used by NASCAR racers. This V8 could handle the power, and featured a cross ram intake manifold. It was good for 635bhp at 6800rpm. There was also the problem of funding. By 1978 Herb Adams' Pontiac Silverbird had entered the similar class SCCA Trans Am Category II. Adams' sponsor was the Appliance Wheel Company. Some critics

The Kemp Cobra II design was largely the work of Bob Riley. The race car hit 212mph at Daytona, and originally used a Gapp & Roush 351C V8. (Courtesy Nathan Petroelje www.roadandtrack.com)

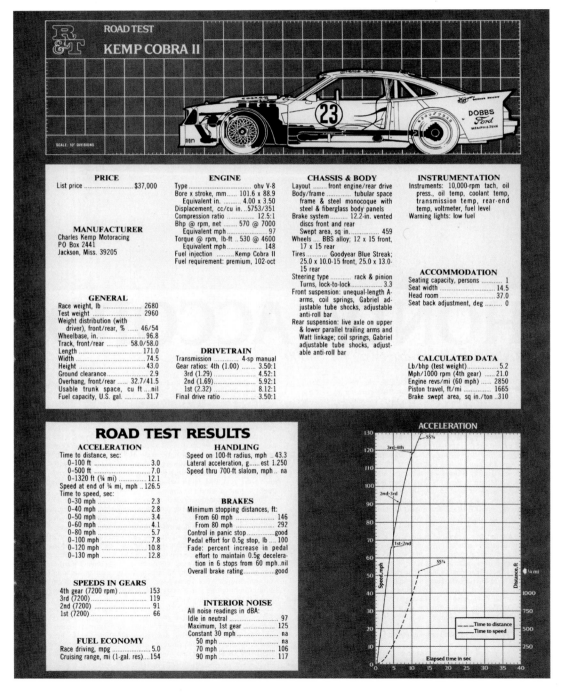

ROAD TEST
KEMP COBRA II
SCALE: 10' DIVISIONS

PRICE
List price $37,000

MANUFACTURER
Charles Kemp Motoracing
PO Box 2441
Jackson, Miss. 39205

GENERAL
Race weight, lb	2680
Test weight	2960
Weight distribution (with driver), front/rear, %	46/54
Wheelbase, in.	96.8
Track, front/rear	58.0/58.0
Length	171.0
Width	74.5
Height	43.0
Ground clearance	2.9
Overhang, front/rear	32.7/41.5
Usable trunk space, cu ft	nil
Fuel capacity, U.S. gal.	31.7

ENGINE
Type	ohv V-8
Bore x stroke, mm	101.6 x 88.9
Equivalent in.	4.00 x 3.50
Displacement, cc/cu in.	5753/351
Compression ratio	12.5:1
Bhp @ rpm, net	570 @ 7000
Equivalent mph	97
Torque @ rpm, lb-ft	530 @ 4600
Equivalent mph	148
Fuel injection	Kemp Cobra II
Fuel requirement: premium, 102-oct	

DRIVETRAIN
Transmission	4-sp manual
Gear ratios: 4th (1.00)	3.50:1
3rd (1.29)	4.52:1
2nd (1.69)	5.92:1
1st (2.32)	8.12:1
Final drive ratio	3.50:1

CHASSIS & BODY
Layout	front engine/rear drive
Body/frame	tubular space frame & steel monocoque with steel & fiberglass body panels
Brake system	12.2-in. vented discs front and rear
Swept area, sq in.	459
Wheels	BBS alloy; 12 x 15 front, 17 x 15 rear
Tires	Goodyear Blue Streak; 25.0 x 10.0-15 front, 25.0 x 13.0-15 rear
Steering type	rack & pinion
Turns, lock-to-lock	3.3
Front suspension: unequal-length A-arms, coil springs, Gabriel adjustable tube shocks, adjustable anti-roll bar	
Rear suspension: live axle on upper & lower parallel trailing arms and Watt linkage; coil springs, Gabriel adjustable tube shocks, adjustable anti-roll bar	

INSTRUMENTATION
Instruments: 10,000-rpm tach, oil press., oil temp, coolant temp, transmission temp, rear-end temp, voltmeter, fuel level
Warning lights: low fuel

ACCOMMODATION
Seating capacity, persons	1
Seat width	14.5
Head room	37.0
Seat back adjustment, deg	0

CALCULATED DATA
Lb/bhp (test weight)	5.2
Mph/1000 rpm (4th gear)	21.0
Engine revs/mi (60 mph)	2850
Piston travel, ft/mi	1665
Brake swept area, sq in./ton	.310

ROAD TEST RESULTS

ACCELERATION
Time to distance, sec:	
0-100 ft	3.0
0-500 ft	7.0
0-1320 ft (¼ mi)	12.1
Speed at end of ¼ mi, mph	126.5
Time to speed, sec:	
0-30 mph	2.3
0-40 mph	2.8
0-50 mph	3.4
0-60 mph	4.1
0-80 mph	5.7
0-100 mph	7.8
0-120 mph	10.8
0-130 mph	12.8

SPEEDS IN GEARS
4th gear (7200 rpm)	153
3rd (7200)	119
2nd (7200)	91
1st (7200)	66

FUEL ECONOMY
Race driving, mpg	5.0
Cruising range, mi (1-gal. res)	154

HANDLING
Speed on 100-ft radius, mph	43.3
Lateral acceleration, g	est 1.250
Speed thru 700-ft slalom, mph	na

BRAKES
Minimum stopping distances, ft:	
From 60 mph	146
From 80 mph	292
Control in panic stop	good
Pedal effort for 0.5g stop, lb	100
Fade: percent increase in pedal effort to maintain 0.5g deceleration in 6 stops from 60 mph	nil
Overall brake rating	good

INTERIOR NOISE
All noise readings in dBA:	
Idle in neutral	97
Maximum, 1st gear	125
Constant 30 mph	na
50 mph	na
70 mph	106
90 mph	117

ACCELERATION
(graph: Speed, mph / Distance, ft vs Elapsed time in sec, with markings 3rd-4th, 2nd-3rd, 1st-2nd, SS¼, SS½)

Time to distance
Time to speed

felt such a sponsor was a back door way for GM to finance a race team, while keeping at a public distance from racing. In any case the Kemp Cobra II was still not FoMoCo supported, and it could have used some help.

The Kemp Cobra II had pace, coming 5th at Ontario in 1976. It eventually got 2nd place, and even secured a pole position, but never won. Those pesky mechanical gremlins always seemed to appear a few laps from the finish. However, the straw that broke the Camel GT's back for Charlie Kemp was continued IMSA opposition to his privateer status. During the 1980 racing season the Kemp Cobra II qualified 20th, but he was denied race participation because IMSA said the car was too slow for its class. However, a factory-backed Foxstang didn't qualify, and was allowed to race anyway!

At the start, authorities felt Kemp Cobra II was an IMSA rulebook breaker, and tried to keep it out. Now in 1980, Charlie Kemp, feeling IMSA's continued bias, decided to withdraw the Kemp Cobra II from the series. By now the Mustang II was no longer in production, and it seemed IMSA preferred to elbow out a privateer with an outmoded model, in favor of the factory outfit racing the current Foxstang.

There was another let down from Kemp's sponsor, dealer Dobbs Ford of Memphis, Tennessee. The parties had a planned deal to offer a street version of the Kemp Cobra II, through Dobbs Ford. Kemp handed over the basic car design, and IMSA copyrighted panels, along with Kemp-tuned suspension, plus special carb and intake manifold. Dobbs built one car, then canned the project. They felt the finished car would be too pricey for commercial volume sales. The imminent arrival of the new 1979 Fox platform Mustang may also have been a factor. The economy was also none too strong in such Carter times. Even DKM pulled the plug on its Macho Trans Am after 1980, in the recessionary wake of the second gas crunch.

Drag racing the Deuce

In the late 1950s Dyno Don Nicholson was one of the first drag racers to utilize a chassis dynamometer to improve performance. He was also ahead of the pack in seeing the potential of Pro Stock (P/S) racing. Outlaw Super Stocks had been really popular in the '60s. It was all about racing vehicles with some semblance of a kinship to normal cars. Dyno Don made a statement to this effect, "The Funny Cars had just gotten too out of hand." For example, Bunny Burkett's 1974 Mustang II Big Cotton Pony BB top alcohol funny car, had little in common with the little Mustang, beyond a body tribute to the mini Deuce.

Dyno Don Nicholson's 1974 Mustang II was the first Mustang II seen in Pro Stock drag racing. (Courtesy Lopez Publications)

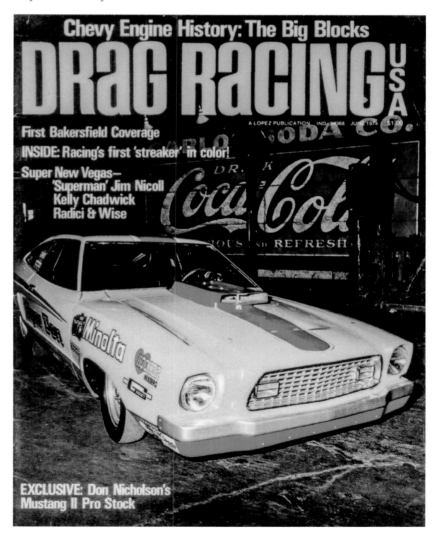

Sitting in his Mustang II, Dyno Don is photographed by Bob McClurg at the once popular Underground Atlanta shopping and entertainment district in Georgia. (Courtesy Lopez Publications)

Don Nicholson might well be described as one of drag racing's "elder statesmen." At the age of 47, he remembers being interested in race cars since he was 12 — a span of 35 years! But there's nothing old about his cars and the way he drives them. In fact, his new Mustang II is the first of its kind. "Dyno Don" first came to the fore in the quarter-mile sport in the heyday of Chevy 409 Super Stocks. In the mid-1960's, he campaigned one of the first fliptop Comets, a forerunner of more modern funny cars. He was also one of the first to recognize the potential of the Pro Stock category, carrying the Ford banner into the P/S wars with a Maverick and later a Winter-nationals-winning Pinto. Now, once more, he's belied his age by introducing an innovative machine based on Ford's sporty subcompact. He chose the fastback version of the popular little Ford for its obvious aerodynamic advantages over the notchback. Don Hardy prepped the chassis, while Earl Wade built the engine, a small-block Ford 351. The powerplant is equipped with Brooks Racing Components rods and 12.3-to-1 pistons on a Delta crank and a General Kinetics roller cam. Wade jobbed out the head porting to Mullen and Company and the balancing to Bill's Speed Shop. A Hays dual-disc clutch and Lenco gearbox transmit power to a set of Schiefer 5.57 rear axle gears in a Ramcharger housing. The axle shafts are Summers Brothers. The unusual photos were taken amidst crowds of curious on-lookers at the famed "Underground Atlanta," Georgia. *continued*

45

Dyno Don's road back to more realistic racing saw a succession of P/S Fords, which led to the World's first P/S Mustang II. Drag Racing USA magazine's June 1974 issue declared the pioneering act of this 1974 racer,"…an innovative machine based on Ford's sporty subcompact." (2) The fastback bodystyle was selected over the notchback, due to the former's better aerodynamics. The car had a Don Hardy prepared chassis. Earl Wade handled the small block 351C. It

Dyno Don's Mustang II, featured a Don Hardy prepared chassis. Hardy's detail work was exemplified, by a 'Dyno-Don' stamp on the 351C's engine bracket. (Courtesy Lopez Publications)

"Dyno Don" moved to Atlanta when match racing was at its peak and the hottest action was on the southern strips. He's since become one of the Georgia city's top racing stars. His best outing so far with his new Mustang II P/S (left) is 8.72 seconds at 154 mph. And there's more where that came from!

Stock 'Stang II body (below) was acid dipped by Aerochem to reduce metal thickness and weight. Doors, front end, lock lid are quick-release fastened. The chassis details (right) offer a fine display of Don Hardy's superb craftsmanship. Look closely at the front engine bracket (above) and you'll see that the metal has been stamped "Dyno-Don." Those big Holleys are on an Edelbrock manifold.

47

had a dual 4 barrel Holley carb set up, on an Edelbrock intake manifold. Inside there lived a General Kinetics roller cam, Brooks Racing Components rods, 12.3:1 CR pistons and Delta crankshaft. Heads were by Mullen & Co. and balancing was carried out by Bill's Speed Shop.

The Lenco gearbox had a Hays dual disc clutch, leading to a Ramcharger diff housing with Schiefer 5.57 rear gears and Summers Brothers axle shafts. The body was acid-dipped by Aerochem to shed weight, and doors, front end, and locklid were quick-release fastened.

Drag Racing USA magazine called Henry's new Deuce a sporty subcompact. Dyno Don Nicholson correctly judged Mustang II fastback, to have an aero advantage over its notchback sibling. (Courtesy Lopez Publications)

Displaying Don Hardy's attention to detail, the front engine bracket was stamped 'Dyno-Don.' By mid '74, Dyno Don's Deuce did an 8.72 second pass at 154mph. In a July 3 1975 match race at the St.Louis International, Dyno Don Nicholson beat Bill 'Grumpy' Jenkins' Chevy Monza, setting an 8.67 second P/S record in the process.

Old school match racing heads up, not handicap style, was real popular. Dyno Don moved to Atlanta, because this was the place to be with match racing at its peak. Southern states' drag venues were the scene of the action, and Dyno Don was mainly into such regional match races. However, in 1977 he did the whole NHRA Nationals series in his Pro Stock Mustang II. He ran out a winner in the Gator Nationals, Spring Nationals and US Nationals.

However, there was one time he didn't win. It was all part of Dyno Don's strategy to secure the 1977 Championship. He qualified low, to limit the 1976 champ Larry Lombardo from scoring maximum points. Dyno Don limited Lombardo, by drawing him and edging him out early in the eliminations. In the 1977 season's points standings Lombardo wound up third, Bob Glidden was second and Dyno Don Nicholson won the championship by 1400 points.

If 1973 belonged to the Gapp & Roush Pinto, then 1974 saw the turn of the team's new Mustang II. Success came with this subcompact too, as seen at the Cecil County Dragway in August 1974. Wayne Gapp won the WAMS All-American Pro Stock Championship, and achieved his second P/S victory at Cecil County. His Mustang II and the "Brooklyn Heavy" Dodge of Herb McCandless were the only two P/S cars entering the 8s that day.

In round one Gapp edged out Iaconio with a 9.25 second pass versus 9.29 seconds at the same 146mph. He defeated Larson in the second round, with an 8.98 second pass at 151mph against a 9.17 second E.T. at 148mph. Ann Cardenti set the classic scene, "Ford versus Chevy – the age old battle pulled to the line for the final." Wayne Gapp beat out Shafiroff with an 8.98 second pass against a 9.04 second ET.

On to the September Denver NHRA WCS, and another Gapp & Roush Mustang II win, saw Wayne Gapp at the top of the series points standing. He seemed a shoe-in for the Pro Stock title. In round one Gapp did a 9.7 second pass at 138.67mph bye run. Round two involved the Gapp & Roush Mustang II doing a 9.65 second pass at 139.31mph. It was a low time and speed for the meet that beat the 9.87 second ET at 138.88mph of Tom Haller's Chevy Vega. In the final, Gapp did

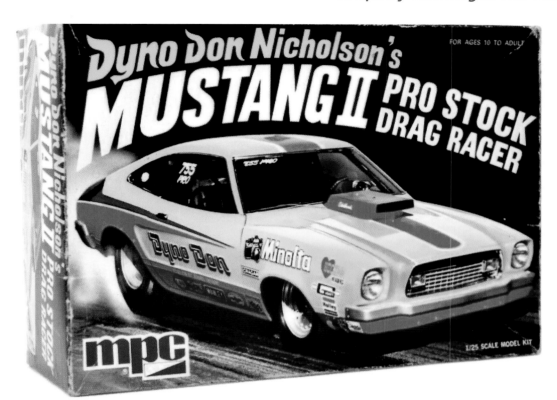

At the age of 50, Dyno Don Nicholson won the 1977 NHRA Pro Stock Winston World Championship title in his Mustang II fastback. (Courtesy round2corp.com)

After an NHRA Pro Stock 1973 World title, Wayne Gapp and Gapp & Roush turned to Mustang II in 1974. (Courtesy Roush Automotive Collection)

Bob Glidden's Pinto narrowly edged out Wayne Gapp's Gapp & Roush Mustang II for the 1974 NHRA P/S World Championship. The Gapp & Roush Mustang II is being restored over 2017-18 by the Roush Automotive Collection. (Courtesy Roush Automotive Collection)

Inspired by those '70s Pro Stockers, Tony Hall's Mustang II Nitemare gives competitors night terrors to. Things can get a mite blurry in the cockpit during a sub-nine second run! (Courtesy Tony Hall)

a 9.66 second run at 134.18mph, beating Kelly Chadwick's Vega.

Match racing was very popular. Underlining this, the Numidia Pennsylvania track hired the best match races to draw the largest crowds. That certainly transpired in October 1974, when Wayne Gapp triumphed over Bill Grumpy Jenkins. The best-of-three race event saw Grumpy Jenkins' 8.82 second pass at 153.58mph edge out Gapp on an 8.79 second pass at 152mph. Bill Jenkins fouled round two, with Wayne Gapp recording a P/S track record 8.61 second pass to Grumpy's 9.06 second ET at 149.50mph. Wayne Gapp's Gapp & Roush Mustang II won round three, setting a new mph track record in the process. His 8.88 second ET at

154.10mph beat Jenkins' 8.79 second ET.

So it seemed the Gapp & Roush Mustang II was going to emulate the success of their '73 season Pinto. However, in stepped Bob Glidden and some bad luck. Glidden had managed a comeback during the '74 race season, who won his final Division 3 race at Bowling Green Kentucky. Then came the season-ending, and very eventful, Super Nationals. During the semis the Gapp & Roush Mustang II lost its fiberglass liftback at 150mph. It flew up 50 feet, and smashed into the ground in a million pieces, or so it seemed. Gapp & Roush got hold of a Hertz rental Mustang II fastback, and raided its steel/glass liftback assembly. It was 100lb heavier than their racing equivalent, but needs

must when Glidden is driving. It looks like that extra weight cost them the hundredth of a second that saw Bob Glidden beat Wayne Gapp to take the 1974 NHRA Pro Stock title in a Pinto.

It seemed that in the '70s the Hertz Rent-A-Car connection didn't help Mustang like it used to. The Gapp & Roush Mustang II was campaigned through the 1975 season. Wayne Gapp then took out an ad: "For Sale Gapp & Roush '74 Mustang II Pro Stock Less Drivetrain. Priced To Sell contact Wayne Gapp 313-425-0640." The car eventually joined the Roush Collection, and was restored during 2017-2018.

Modifying Mustang II

It's unfortunate that Mustang II's reputation often precedes it, because it closes peoples' minds to the idea of modification for higher performance. However, like the later Foxstang, the Mustang II V8 is roughly 3200lb, and powered by one of the 20th Century's great high-performance engines, so why not? Unusually for any car, all of the Mustang II's powerplants were very good engines. However, admittedly in this timeframe and marketing region, they weren't at their best.

In Europe the Ford Sierra RS Cosworth used the 2-liter Pinto I4 to make over 200bhp, and reach nearly 150mph. In North America, the Lima-engined Merkur XR4Ti cousin was also a strong performer. Similarly, there were a number of European tuners like Janspeed, that turboed the 2.8-liter Cologne V6 in the Sierra XR4i. Enough straight line acceleration was produced to frighten a Lamborghini Countach. That said, the easiest course of action with Mustang II, is to focus on the V8 cars.

It's also wise to concentrate on improving the automatic-equipped Mustang II V8s. The 4-speed cars used the European-sourced Type-E gearbox. This was a light shifting, close-ratio device that could cope with Mustang II's stock 302, but couldn't handle much

more torque. It was also not easy to fit an HD 4-speed because of space limitations. The stock set up has a 10in clutch and 11in flywheel. Going to a bigger box means no room for a nice set of headers. It's tight on Mustang II between the bell housing and frame rails. However, the C4 automatic used on Mustang II V8 does have the 11in flywheel. This box can be built up to handle the power of a very potent Windsor small block.

The sky is the limit with the 302 V8, with an aftermarket bigger than the Grand Canyon. Along more modest lines, going for a 600 CFM 4-barrel carb on an aftermarket dual plane intake manifold wakes things up compared to the stock 2-barrel and single plane set up. The '83 Foxstang GT 5.0 used a 600 CFM Holley 4-barrel to good effect. Ford's SVO hydraulic sports cam No. M-6250-A312 offers 290 degree intake duration and 0.496 in exhaust valve lift. For a combo that works, the cam should be combined with the M-6500-A303 set of lifters.

Aside from Pro Stock Pintos and Mustang IIs, Hooker Headers did a set for street Mustang II V8s. This set carried the part number 6120. The above-mentioned complete package would boost the 302 from around 130-140bhp net to 210-220bhp net. That's about equal to the final 1994 injected 5.0 GT Foxstangs. The Mustang II would have improved its ET by a couple of seconds to be a low 15s car, or quicker than a '68 Torino GT 390. To cope with power gains, a change from the stock 8 in differential would be wise. Mustang II shares the same 43in leaf spring perch to perch measurement as the 1965-70 Mustangs. However, it only matches the 1965-66 Mustangs for axle flange to flange 52¼in measurement. The 1967-70 cars were 2in wider because Ford set the Mustang up to accept a big-block V8.

The idea is to raid the Mustang One's parts shelf for go faster goodies. In the late '70s and into the 1980s, company Total Performance made an engine mount package for the Mustang II, so it could accept the 351C or 351W V8s. To help with traction, braking as well as reducing front-end float and body roll, tire, rim and suspension upgrades are possible. All going beyond the stock 13in related hardware. Car Craft magazine modified a '78 King Cobra, and tried a set of 14 x 6in alloys with E 60 radial tires. Such rolling stock fitted with no inner panel fender work, and resembled the Turbo Cast rim combo used on late '70s AMC AMXs, except the Ford retained the Mustang II's four-bolt mounting.

In the early '80s, Addco of Florida had upgrade parts for Mustang II. There was a 1in front swaybar (part no 875), part no 345 was an Addco rear 7/8 in swaybar for Mustang IIs with no stock rear swaybar. Addco offered a 7/8 in rear bar, to replace the factory Competition Suspension rear swaybar (Addco part no 346). The Florida company also did a set of gas pressure shocks, part no 4511 (front). For Mustang IIs built on or before Nov 5 1973, rear shocks carried the part no 5515. Part no 5523 covered Mustang IIs after that date.

As a sign of the Mustang II's potential, Car Craft also played with the King Cobra's engine. Out of the box it did a 17 second flat ¼ mile at 80.6mph. With Holley 4-barrel and Hooker headers it was down to 16.7

seconds. Open headers lowered the time to 15.9 seconds at 88mph. There was a lot of tune up potential with these smogger 302s. As observed by *Road Test* in April 1975, the Mustang II was strong in 0-50mph, but tailed off thereafter. However, when the stats aren't right, start modifying!

Mustang II Monroe Handler

Hot rodding and car customization are an American tradition. It started in the U.S.A. as a natural flow on from mass production. When Henry Ford said you could have any color, as long as it was black, some people decided to personalize their car by painting it red, white and maybe blue. With mass production you are also going to quickly have a stock of cheap used cars to tinker with. Famous examples are a 1000 horsepower T-bucket called Andromeda, and the Pete Chapouris built California Kid. The latter was a flamed '34 Ford Model A coupe that became a silver screen sensation in the movie *The California Kid*.

In an example of reverse history, the popularity of Pinto and Mustang II, saw such cars raided for chassis hardware parts. Such mechanical bounty was then bestowed upon hot rod project cars in the 1970s-90s era. It's nice to keep one's T-bucket and '32 Deuce all Blue Oval.

The 1977 Mustang II Monroe Handler represented perhaps the ultimate customized Mustang II. (Courtesy Tony Hall)

The Monroe Handler represented the combined efforts of *Hot Rod* magazine, Creative Car Craft (CCC), Harris Dynamics, and Monroe! (Courtesy Tony Hall)

However, in 1977 the Mustang II got a customized job that was all its own. This car was showcased in a popular national magazine, and also appeared in print ads. The car was the Mustang II Monroe Handler. The Monroe Handler had the biggest names in the industry involved: *Hot Rod* magazine, Dave Wacko Kent, Gapp & Roush and Monroe of course. All for Dearborn's modern Deuce.

The Monroe Handler represented the ideas of *Hot Rod*, and product promotion for Monroe. The car was a modified Mustang II fastback V8, with strong connection to the car one could actually buy. Indeed, for a time it was possible to create your own Monroe Handler. It was the cover car of the June 1977 issue

of *Hot Rod* magazine, with its chassis and engine covered in the August and September 1977 issues respectively. Stylistically, the car was the product of a winning *Hot Rod* competition sketch, with refinements added by Harry Bradley, Tod Gerstenburger, and Harry Weeks.

To build the grand design, the services of Creative Car Craft (CCC), were sought. The company was run by Dave "Wacko" Kent, and team members that included Don Borth and Charlie Eddy. With 300 hours of very skilled work, they turned a normal fastback into a steel-bodied modified Monroe Handler. The body had a distinctive blended front spoiler complex, and integrated rear spoiler too. Swept up sides continued into the rear fenders. As usually happens with such projects, there was an intention to make a bodykit for later sale. Molds were taken of the panels, to create a $1000 fiberglass bodykit.

The fiberglass front fascia would bolt onto the stock Mustang II sheetmetal. The rear part of the kit was glued on. The spoiler and front flared fenders

In addition to the original steel-bodied 363ci Windsor-V8-powered Monroe Handler, Monroe commissioned six replicas. These were normal fastbacks fitted with the CCC fiberglass kit and cosmetic trim. (Courtesy Tony Hall)

were bolt-ons, with provision for stock bumpers to stay. Rear kit additions would be epoxyied onto the quarter panels, with room for the normal rear bumper. In keeping with the times, a roof mounted CB (Citizen's Band) radio antenna was present. The fastback was visually resplendent in Monroe's iconic yellow. It wore 4-bolt, 14in Centerline disc wheels, wrapped in GR50-14 B F Goodrich T/A Radials.

This official Monroe replica has been modified with: 302 4bbl/C4 auto power team, Heidts tubular front end, subframe connectors, dual side exhausts, and 17in Legend Centerline rims. The ram air hood is functional. With back seat delete, this Mustang II takes a back seat to no one! (Courtesy Tony Hall)

The chassis mods were handled by Trevor Harris' Californian concern Harris Dynamics. The objective was to create a nice, usable street car. Working with stock hardware, there would be a kit for Mustang IIs that would work with stock ride height and tires if necessary. So stock rubber insulators and travel limiters were retained. A flat rear second leaf spring was tried, but abandoned. The stock rear swaybar was also kept – the aim was minimal disruption. However, a 1⅛in front swaybar was added, and Monroe's Dick Arend helped with the selection of Monroe Handler street series shocks.

The Monroe Handler was dropped 2½in at the front, and 1½in at the rear. Stock Centerline rim offsets were used. The rims were 8in wide front and 9in wide rearwards. Some inner panel work was needed, to stop slight rubbing on full steering lock. Engine wise, it was a case of a Gapp & Roush Windsor 363 small-block stroker, with cast iron nodular 351 Cleveland crank, plus various Gapp & Roush trick pieces. There was only 38 degrees of advance at 3600rpm, so the motor could work on low octane pump gas. Monroe Handler was very practical!

The original steel-bodied car and 6 Monroe commissioned copies went on tour in the second half of 1977. A specially built trailer would take the cars to 130 shows, plus major races like the Indy 500. Revell also had a ¹⁄₂₅ scale model planned for late 1977 release. Monroe print ads featuring the Monroe Handler had a Revell order coupon that could be mailed to get the kit. The 6 commissioned copies featured the fiberglass CCC kit (part no ccp 200), and normal '78 MY Mustang power teams. The ccp 200 kit was still available from Dave Kent's company in 1982. Earlier on it was possible to order the flares and spoilers separately.

Mustang II King Cobra – the first 5.0

It's usually thought the 5.0 era started with the 1982 Mustang GT. However, the first Mustang to wear this sacred metric designation callout was the 1978 Mustang II King Cobra. The model, a one

By 1978 Henry's Cobra was getting some bite back. The '78 only King Cobra could match the acceleration of the new Porsche 928 V8 automatic. (Courtesy Christopher Hoexum www.grautogallery.com)

In the August '78 issue of *Cars*, Don Chaikin considered King Cobra's dashboard monstrously big. However, it had to be large to fit Mustang II's excellent HVAC system. By 1978, Cobra II matched King Cobra's absence of door card metal trim. (Courtesy Christopher Hoexum www. grautogallery.com)

year only visual/performance package, was never marketed, or spoken of as a 'Five-Point-Oh,' but that's sometimes how things start. The very first BMW M sedan often had the 'M' badge overlooked. '5.0' just didn't mean anything to anyone in 1978. Indeed, the whole idea of a reverse hoodscoop, metric callout decal and animal hood graphic was influenced by the wildly popular '70s Pontiac Trans Am. Many were impressed by that car's '6.6-litre' decal callout. In the August 1978 issue of *Cars*, Don Chaikin said King Cobra resembled a "quasi-Trans Am."

Many cars of the era were following the sales success that was the Bandit Trans Am. AMC did something similar too with the reborn 1977-80 AMX. A big hood graphic and brushed metal interior trim. Even the Nissan/Datsun Gazelle tried a similar animal hood graphic, with black and gold livery a popular choice. Today, the Trans Am is long gone from new car price lists, but the 5.0 continues

with the modern Coyote V8. It pays tribute to Windsor V8s of yore.

The past blended with the present. This was what cars like the Trans Am and King Cobra were starting in the late '70s. A big engine size hoodscoop display harked back to muscle cars past. However, the metric callout spoke of a contemporary, European sophistication that Detroit was on the path towards. There was much discussion of this 'new age' muscle car in the January 13 1978 issue of *Autoweek*. The article was titled "Ford and Pontiac bring back the racer look." Note that at this time Z/28 and Corvette were in the wilderness, and were seldom mentioned. However, in any given year, the Mustang nameplate couldn't be ignored.

The universal message from Trans Am, King Cobra and AMX was that these cars were not like the tire fryers of yesteryear. They were sporty, personal coupes, with equal measures of V8 performance, handling and luxury. All

Retuned to 250lb/ft at only 1600rpm, the King Cobra 5.0 could show a clean pair of hoofs to many a late '70s disco delight! (Courtesy Christopher Hoexum www.grautogallery.com)

in keeping with the image and status conscious times. Ford Marketing Plans manager, Don Cook, described King Cobra's raison d'etre. It was a logical follow up to the successful Cobra II, which was still available in 1978. Compared to Cobra II, King Cobra was the same, only more so. A step further in creating a powerful appearing car, an image making 2+2 coupe if you will. Cook admitted that federal laws, such as CAFE and smog inspections, meant that the new performance cars couldn't functionally equal their unemcumbered '60s forebears, "but it is comparable to other muscle cars on the road today, like the Firebird." Don Cook said there was a conscious move with King Cobra, to satisfy the performance buyer of 1978. All FoMoCo's best stuff was put in one model. Cook said that included their strongest engine.[3]

Ford admitted a buyer could add King Cobra's performance goodies individually to a $3877 Mustang II 2+2 fastback. However, buyers had changed. They no longer wished to go through pages of order blanks, like in olden times. They had got used to accessory groups bringing together similar options. They were also beyond the days of ordering a hot motor, poverty interior and dog bowl hubcaps. No sir, they preferred a snazzy,

stand-alone package with a name, like King Cobra. The moniker was shorthand for a speedy and luxurious ride. In this regard, King Cobra was more akin to Mustang II Mach I. One could get a four-cylinder motor with Cobra II. However, Mach I and King Cobra brought a certain collection under one hood. And there was a lot included for the loot.

Visually, King Cobra had a Cobra snake hood graphic, reverse hoodscoop with single spear stripe, and King Cobra door callouts. The King Cobra name was repeated on the rear deck. Fashionable matte black featured on front grille, headlight doors, taillight surrounds, window outline and B-pillar band. There were black trim accents on bumpers, rear deck and black surrounds for the side marker lights. Pinstriping followed the window line, fenders, roof and rear deck trunk liftback.

Functionally forged Lacy alloys, power steering, power brakes, HD suspension, HD cooling and the latest 139bhp 302 V8 were all standard. Dashboard brushed metal trim was included under King Cobra special trim, but like '78 Cobra II these metal accents were no longer on door card trims. A console was still optional! Unusually the leatherette-trimmed 3-spoke sports steering wheel was optional too, but was probably fitted to the 4318 King Cobras built. And it all almost didn't happen.

Don Cook mentioned that the King Cobra project was on, then off and finally on again. In 1977 the main considered name for the new Cobra II Plus model was Starga. King Cobra was a side bet. One King Cobra prototype was shown in the summer of 1977. Mechanically it was consistent with the eventual King Cobra, including a 1090 steel rear swaybar for the car's HD suspension. However, this proto had more elaborate pinstriping – Von Dutch on acid – and a deeper snow plow-like front spoiler. The latter probably invoking memories of the late '60s NASCAR Aero Wars.

Over twice the trunk capacity of a GM F-body coupe. However, the hatchback format implied more bodyflex than the Mustang II notchback. (Courtesy Christopher Hoexum www.grautogallery.com)

Three or four different proposals were considered before the project was reactivated in the fall of 1977. Then started a crash program to try and make the original release date. The rest of the 1978 Mustang II range, including revised Cobra II, had been launched early to boost Mustang sales, which worked. Ford people had originally hoped to get late year sales with King Cobra. As things eventuated, the King Cobra missed its original projected release date by only one week. The December dealer reaction to King Cobra was very positive. The press were mostly on King Cobra's side too.

Hot Rod magazine had been a champion of the Mustang II cause. The journal ran major stories on the Monroe Handler in the 1977 June, August and September issues. In the October '77 issue it ran the story 'Meet the King,' probably motivated by the very recent passing of Elvis Presley. The article was about the magazine's experience of the summer '77 Dearborn King Cobra preview. *Hot Rod* loved the concept and declared without reservation: "…the newest, most eye-appealing Mustang model yet … "

The 1978 Mustang II King Cobra, was the first Mustang to carry the '5.0' designation. It did so on its reverse hoodscoop. (Courtesy www. forgottenpony.com)

Autoweek were more cautious in January 1978, stating: "Pleasant, with reservations." The publication thought the 302 engine was great, plenty of power, but pondered the tach's redline absence. We do know Ford really wanted a rotary engine in the early '70s, but this was too much! Reservations concerned the car's handling on imperfect surfaces. The problem of axle tramp and getting bumped off line were common to all sporty, live axle Detroit Demonmobiles. It was even true for Corvette, surely the only IRS car in history to ride like a live-axled machine.

This customized '78 King Cobra has Screaming Yellow exterior, factory decals and pinstripes, custom blackout grille, shaved door handles, and 17in Boyd Coddington Crown Jewel wheels. (Courtesy Angie)

Don Chaikin echoed this ride/ handling problem in *Cars* magazine. The King Cobra drew comments that mirrored the final C3 Vettes. Basically, a body structure lacking rigidity, allied to very firm suspension. It was a recipe for shake, rattle but minimal roll off glass-smooth freeways. Cars of the King Cobra, Corvette, Trans Am and Z/28's ilk polarized opinion. Some liked 'em rough and ready. A street fighter with good 'ol smooth and vocal V8 voice. Others were getting into the European camp of an all-road-conditions handler. Riverside or refined, the choice was yours.

Mustang II & Foxstang – Cobra to Cobra

Don Chaikin's King Cobra evaluation in *Cars* noted that Ford's new pony attracted plenty of attention from the high school and burger joint crowd. He asked if all the attention, or the King Cobra surcharge, was worth it? Ten years earlier such questions would never have arisen. The enthusiastic pony car buyer would have simply asked, where can

I sign up? However, now people were making valued judgements about cars that used to be just for fun. If one had to ask, the King Cobra was in the 6 to 7 grand ballpark, and undercut a 6.6-liter Trans Am by $2500.

The question was academic, because hot on the King Cobra's heels, or hoofs, came the all-new Fairmont-based 1979 Fox platform third generation Mustang. The new car looked very different. It was modern in a slightly wedge-shaped European fashion. Mustang II critics were elated – the visual change made them think a corner had been turned. However, under the skin, Mustang was still a rear-drive, live-axled sporty car, based upon a humble sedan.

The Foxstang was a very good, high selling, affordable high-performance car. However, like the C1 Corvette, it took a few years to find itself. In the 1979-81 era, a contest with the outgoing Mustang II was somewhat of a draw. The Cobra visual package continued, and in 1979 alone so did the 302 V8. Now just called Mustang Cobra V8, the new car rose to 140bhp – a gain of one. Major attention was on the new TRX wheel/tire system. It was a combination of metric-sized 4-bolt rim and tire that promised a whole greater than the sum of its parts, but results were mixed.

The TRX Michelin system brought improved ride, bigger rims and better transient response. That said, it wasn't too hot with off the line traction, or short braking distances. It was also very expensive concerning replacement tires.

The Roush-built 5.0 has dual Edelbrock carbs, Performer Air Gap intake manifold, and chrome accents. It's joined to a C4 auto with shift kit. A three core race radiator with dual Flex-A-Lite fans, keeps things cool. A polished independent rear suspension helps put down the power. (Courtesy Angie)

Inside, custom embroidered crowned Cobras feature, complemented by yellow piping and stitching. Outside, Stumpy's subframe connectors and slotted rotors gripped by Wilwood calipers keep King Cobra safe. (Courtesy Angie)

When Don Chaikin tested the King Cobra, he found cornering was only limited by the 13in tires rolling off the rims. He wished for Pirelli P7s. Either way, Mustang was a few years away from the 16 in SVO hardware. The Ford Fairmont

was designed in a post fuel crisis environment, so weight saving was key. In turn, the Foxstang was a good 150lb lighter than the Mustang II. Enthusiasts use Kurt Stumpf subframe connectors on Mustang II. On Foxstang, chassis flex is slightly worse. The first job anyone does before adding serious power is to beef up Foxstang's unibody. In 1980 and 1981, the 302 V8 was absent. FoMoCo, and many others, thought V8s were on the way out. After the second fuel crisis, it pushed the turbo 2.3 Lima as the performance engine.

During the 1980-81 era, the Mustang Cobra V8 was limited to the 255ci econo-eight, rated at 119 and 120bhp for the two years respectively. *Road & Track* recorded 16.3 seconds for the ¼ mile in the 1982 Mustang GT 5.0. *Cars'* August 1978 time for Mustang II King Cobra was 16.59 seconds. Objectively, it wasn't until 1983 when the Mustang GT came forth with a Holley 4-barrel-fed 302, and terrific BW T-5 5-speeder, that the new Fox platform Mustang reached full gallop. Unfortunately for the car that saved the Mustang nameplate, Mustang II, there has been muted praise.

It was at the 2009 Tradex Show, in Abbotsford BC, that George Barris and Chip Foose came over at their own volition to sign this King Cobra's radiator support cover. (Courtesy Angie)

Mustang II came at a time when Detroit's critics said the home-grown product was too big, too thirsty, didn't handle and was poorly built. Mustang II addressed all those concerns, and sold a 1,107,718 total. When Wayne Gapp spoke to *Super Stock* and *Drag Illustrated* in October 1975 about Joe Ruggirello's Sudden Death street racer, he just called it a Mustang. In August 1975, *Motor Trend*'s Herb L. Adams said: "Ford's Mustang II (hopefully, it will be called simply 'Mustang' in the future) is an excellent all around car. If the original Mustang and Foxstang weren't quite as good in some areas as memory and folklore tell us, maybe Mustang II wasn't that bad? One thing is for certain, my little pony is a Mustang too!"

The signatures of George Barris and Chip Foose join a famous hardware list on this King Cobra, including Roush, Edelbrock and Eagle headers. (Courtesy Angie)

The Mustang II V8 revived the sporty spirit of the original T-Bird! (Courtesy Marc Cranswick)

The rise of the small car, 1945-70

After World War II, the American public were ready for fresh, new car designs. Unfortunately, early pickings were just warmed-over prewar jobs. Studebaker declared it was first by far, with a postwar car, and 1950 turned out to be its best year. Very quickly, Detroit's Big Three mobilized their resources and satisfied the public's appetite, turning Detroit into the Motor City in the process. Larger, more lavish cars, and modern overhead-valve V8 engines for family cars arrived by the mid-1950s. However, the glee club soon disbanded.

A poster child for the late '50s recession was the poor Edsel. Edsel represented Ford and corporate America overreaching, in terms of what the public wanted or could afford. Even before the economic crisis, sales of small cars were gaining ground. They were being provided almost exclusively by European companies. Dafs, Fiats, Renault etc, and, most prominently, the VW Beetle. Detroit was never really interested in this segment.

Too small, too cheap and not enough mark up, so not even the dealers liked them. The Kaiser Henry J sold a fair few, the Nash Metropolitan was snazzier and did somewhat better. However, once again, Detroit wasn't really interested. After all, America was a big country, going places in more ways than one. Dinah Shore sang *See the USA in your Chevrolet*. She didn't sing buy an import, break down and seek a shade tree mechanic. Americans didn't like small cars ... or did they?

Funnily enough, a Nash Metropolitan was featured in the final season of TV's *Starsky & Hutch*. In the episodes 'Targets without badges,' the police duo resign after failing to protect a witness. Hutch then turned up in that colorful two-tone confection, known as 'The Met.' Well, he never really dug Starsky's Striped Tomato. The Met did good business in the late '50s recession. Ford's response to the recession, courtesy of new leader Robert Strange McNamara, was to can the Edsel and introduce the all-new compact 1960 Falcon. The Falcon's target was the

3

Ford Pinto: Dearborn's own subcompact

At its peak, VW used the Bug to grab 70% of the imported car market. Lee Iacocca used the Pinto as Ford's pest control! On '71 MY Pintos, a three-speed auto ($175) and factory a/c ($370) were options for 2-liter cars only. (Courtesy Marc Cranswick)

To commemorate the 1972 Munich Olympic games, Ford did a Sprint cosmetic package for Pinto, Maverick and Mustang. A 1976 follow-up pack called Stallion, was offered on the same three model lines. A white 1971 Pinto sedan was a US embassy car in the 1983 TV movie *Saigon: Year Of The Cat*, with E G Marshall. (Courtesy Ford Motor Company www.ford.com)

We've come a long way from basic black.

1926 Ford Model T Coupe.

1972 Ford Pinto Runabout with Sprint Decor Option.

If you find yourself staring whenever you see a Model "T" go by, we don't blame you. It was some kind of car. (Even if it did come mostly in black.) It was simple. It was tough. And if something went wrong, you could probably fix it with a screwdriver and a pair of pliers.

Pinto has many of those same qualities. Which is good to know if you're the kind of person who likes cars, and likes to work on them. Pinto is the kind of car you _can_ work on, without having to be some kind of master mechanic. It's also a car you can work with. There are lots of things you can

add—both from Pinto's list of options and from the specialty equipment people. If you start with the Sprint Option we've shown, you don't even have to start with basic black.

Sprint Decor Group includes the following equipment: Red, White and Blue Exterior Accents. Trim Rings with Color-Keyed Hubcaps. Dual Racing Mirrors. Red, White and Blue Cloth and Vinyl Bucket Seats. Full Carpeting. Deluxe 2-Spoke Steering Wheel. Stars and Stripes Decal. A78 x 13 White Sidewall Tires. Blackout Grille.

When you get back to basics, you get back to Ford.

Better idea for safety...buckle up!

FORD PINTO

FORD DIVISION

VW Beetle. For this reason, McNamara wanted Falcon to have four cylinders.

Robert McNamara wasn't much into the extravagance that led to Edsel, he believed in statistics and efficiency. The four-banger would have cost Ford $13.50 less to make per car too. McNamara liked that, so would have Henry Ford. Back in the days of the Model T, the wooden crates used to ship CKD Model Ts were used as floorboards when the cars were assembled. Henry Ford was more snug than Jack Benny!

The tightness went well with Detroit's attitude to economy small cars. They were very basic transport, low cost and sometime soon the prospect would want and could afford something better. Fortunately, McNamara was persuaded the Falcon would sell better with six cylinders. This opened the hood to the compact's 144ci and 170ci I6s.

The press judged Falcon to be a very plain car, reflective of McNamara personally. Not much good could have come from this lark, if you pardon the pun. Even Studebaker offered a V8 in its recession-winning compact. However, the Falcon was a tremendous success, so too its new 1960 compact rivals the Chevy Corvair and the Plymouth Valiant. It seemed Americans did like smaller cars, if they were designed with North American conditions in mind. History shows the Falcon, Corvair and Valiant saw off the European small car imports, except for one.

In the 1978 movie *The Betsy*, the patriarch of the fictitious car giant Bethlehem Motors, said he was beaten to the market by the two biggest SOBs in history, Henry Ford and Adolf Hitler! Now, Bethlehem Motors was going to introduce a revolutionary small car to take the world into the fuel efficient '80s, called The Betsy. Harold Robbins' story was correct: Ford and Hitler were hard taskmasters, both behind successful, affordable cars. In 1972 the Beetle overtook the Model T's production record as the biggest seller of all time. It partly got there on strong American market sales.

North American Bug sales were past 100,000 in 1960, 200,000 in 1963 and 300,000 in 1967. All the while Detroit management were deeply perplexed. Why would folks want a small, cramped, slow and noisy car, whose styling never changed? Aside from truly small size and easy driving, Robert Schilling offered explanations in the April 1967 issue of *Motor Trend*. A good base product that continually evolved, aggressive marketing and an expanding parts/service network that actually worked. So how does the man who drives the snowplow get to work? He certainly doesn't drive an unreliable Austin 1100!

During 1965 to 1970 the Beetle wasn't alone. Some of the Europeans like Renault and Fiat lingered on, and there were the new Japanese imports. The shovel nose Toyota Corona quickly became a relatively common sight. With a claimed 30mpg and $1760 1967 sticker, it was enticing. With a dual-carb 96 horse I4, the Datsun 1600 had four on the floor and front disk brakes. When Paul Newman got a taste for car racing when preparing for the

To match VW Beetle, Lee Iacocca set limits of 2000 pounds and 2000 bucks for the Pinto's debut. A 1973 Pinto Country Squire wagon is displayed. (Courtesy City View Classic Cars, Texas)

At 69.4in wide, the Pinto's interior supplied the width American buyers preferred. A Luxury Décor Group option also provided plushness absent in many small imports. (Courtesy City View Classic Cars, Texas)

1969 movie *Winning*, he started racing a Datsun 1600. In the movie it was all NASCAR Torinos, and his character drove a T-Bird. The Japanese contingent rose in popularity for the same reasons VW did. Like the Beetle, they were well-made and reliable.

In the meantime American compacts had grown, become more lavish, and by '67 MY all had V8 options, even American Motors. To cater to buyers looking for the smaller cars, the Big Three relied on captive imports sourced from their overseas subsidiaries. The Opel Kadett L and Rallye were sold and serviced by 1300 Buick dealers, more than even VW. The small car imports varied in their suitability for the US market. VW initially did well because, being autobahn bred, the Bug coped well with freeway driving, and the rear-engined/rear-drive format gave good winter snowbelt traction.

Ford seemed well-placed with the British Ford Cortina. Ford ads said: "Introducing another bright idea from Ford … Ford's Model C. Car enthusiasts – their ladies, too – will admire these standard features in the Cortina GT." With its rally stripes and over 90mph top speed, the second generation Cortina seemed ideal. At 168in long, and 65in wide, it was much bigger than some imports.

With the close design relationship between the Big Three and their overseas companies, Cortina GT had a familiar late '60s Detroit 'party animal' look and feel. Plymouth tried something similar with their Cricket (Hillman Avenger). However, were the captive imports enough? Not all Ford dealers handled the Cortina. The plan was 650 outlets by the end of 1967. Some of these dealers also sold the UK-supplied Ford Anglia. The Anglia, Cortina and I6-powered Falcon/Mustang, were Ford USA's small economy car selection.[4]

The Ford Pinto wagon made its debut, on February 24 1972. Standard features ran to the bigger 2-liter inline four, front disk brakes/HD rear drums, plus flip open rear quarter windows. This wagon, was one of the 484,512 '73 MY Pintos sold. (Courtesy City View Classic Cars Phone:817-292-4477)

Although VW kept updating the Beetle, one car can't continue forever. The new Japanese designs had more space for passengers and their luggage. Datsuns and Toyotas were also more fashionable, frugal and fast. Pretty soon 'made in Japan' became a mark of quality, and the Japanese automakers took ownership of the North American small car market. VW never regained its small car King status in America. Not even with the Westmoreland-built Rabbit, which suffered several quality control snafus early on.

The domestics had a fight on their hands – it was 1960 all over again. The Big Three would have to come up with American-designed and made, subcompact responses for 1970. Chrysler were sitting this dance out. The smallest member of the Big Three lacked cash, and considered subcompacts a passing fad. AMC stepped in to deliver America's first subcompact on April Fool's Day 1970. Chevrolet chimed in with the 1971 model year Vega. Ford arrived a day later with its new small car.

The very quick Pinto plan

By the start of the '70s, the North American small car market was one million units strong, so the need to have a replacement for the Cortina MkII captive import was great. Planning for the Pinto started in the summer of 1967. The project was being actively worked on from August 1968. That year Robert Eidschun oversaw the design of Pinto's unique shape. Ford's Product Planning Committee

gave approval in December 1968. The Ford Board of Directors formally signed off on the car in January 1969.

Many groups were involved with the project, but there was one single Ford person with major influence on this crucial subcompact, Lee Iacocca. The Pinto was known internally as 'Lee's Car.' With a focus on Pinto's rivals, Iacocca set design limits of 2000lb and $2000. Along with the rest of top management, he ordered a rapid crash program. With time being so tight, several processes had to be done concurrently. The $200 million tooling and car development were done simultaneously.

It all seemed to come together in a 'go to whoa' record that ain't never been beat: 25 months! With time being of the essence, and teething problems with the structural integrity of alternate bodystyles, Ford concentrated solely on the Pinto two-door sedan for the 1970 September 11 market release. Dimensionally, this subcompact sedan was 163in long, 69.4in wide and 50.1in tall. It sat on a 94in wheelbase. American buyers have always appreciated more interior space. So, Pinto was wider than the European small car norm. This included the defunct MkII Cortina.

The narrow track and tall height of small imports like the Mazda 1200 and Simca could make for nervous handling. It was difficult to keep a straight path with the rear-engined French car at a freeway 60-65mph, even without sidewinds. This was why Pinto had a 55in track, front and back! It was also mentioned in the Pinto's

The Pinto Country Squire mimicked the upscale, faux wood-paneled nature of Ford's large Country Squire wagons. The Pinto's namesake was a pony with white and solid color patches. Following the wagon trail of Mustang and Maverick, Pinto continued Ford's equine nameplate lineage. (Courtesy City View Classic Cars, Texas)

early TV ad, that 'The Little Carefree Car' didn't get blown around, like some of the small imports. There was also an absence of the wild rear-engine-induced oversteer found on Beetles.

Pinto was purely conventional with unequal length A-arms up front, coils and shocks. At the rear, it was Detroit's old standby: a leaf-sprung live axle and tube shocks. Somewhat unconventionally, the Pinto became the first mass-produced American car with rack and pinion steering. It was a manual

Billed as 'The Little Carefree Car,' the hatchback version of the Ford Pinto made its debut at the Chicago Auto Show. The European-inspired hatch was dubbed the Runabout, and Henry Ford II had one himself! (Courtesy www.duncanimports.com)

system with 4.2 turns lock to lock. For power teams, FoMoCo combined its all-new design with the proven Ford of Europe Kent 1.6-liter I4 (Ford UK), and the Hummer four-speed (Ford Germany).

The 98ci Kent had been seen in the Cortina. It was rated at 75bhp and 96lb/ft, in gross ratings. *Road & Track* was in favor of the overhead valve Kent, and equally sturdy Hummer four-speed. The Hummer was linked to the early '60s Ford UK Dagenham four-speed. It had a pleasant shift action, and could handle 205lb/ft. This was enough to cope with the Pinto's optional engine, the new EAO 'Pinto' four-cylinder. The inline four-banger was designed for the new Pinto, and had five main bearings for durability and smoothness. It featured both cast iron block and head. The latter had a single overhead cam layout. The Pinto 2-liter, or 122ci, made 100bhp at 5600rpm and 120lb/ft at 3600rpm. EAO I4 had an 8.6:1 CR and drank regular gas. The optional automatic was the Bordeaux C3 three-speed unit, sometimes called Selectshift, and other times referred to by the Cruise-O-Matic handle.

Pinto & rivals

At a glance Pinto seemed mechanically similar to its domestic rivals Chevy Vega and AMC Gremlin. All three were rear-drive small cars of similar size, with a live axle. However, beyond that point, each represented a very different approach to the American subcompact. Gremlin was first out of the blocks, with a design very close to the AMC Hornet. It was basically a truncated compact, with new rear razorback styling, plus the usual range of domestic sixes.

Vega was like a mini 2nd gen Camaro. It had the convenience of a full liftback, and placed its reliance on a single engine. That was a linerless bore, aluminum block SOHC I4. Of the three newcomers, the Pinto possessed the most European character. In fact, in its September 1970 issue, *Car and Driver* called Pinto: "An American-Made Foreign Sedan."[5] Aside

from Ford Europe power teams, Pinto had standard buckets, four on the floor, and soon a hatchback. It didn't look American, and contrasted with Vega's pony car like fastback silhouette. It may have been reverse Europeanization, since the Pinto engine would prove a Ford Europe mainstay into the late 1980s. The thing of it is, next to Gremlin and Vega, the Pinto looked kind of … foreign.

Ford's Pinto seemed to have an edge in key areas concerning power team efficiency. Its overall gas mileage matched the highway cruise figures of six-cylinder Gremlin. With the Hummer four-speed, the Pinto 2-liter had enough zip to better AMC's 232ci machine. The fuel crisis hadn't happened yet, but in an economy car McNamara's desire for a four-banger seemed justified. There was the inconvenience of having to stop for

gas. Gremlin had a 21 gallon tank, versus Pinto's 11 gallons, and combined with a tall 2.73 rear axle, the I6's greater thirst was compensated by cruising range.

Chevy's Vega came with a larger 2.3-liter motor, but was still slower and thirstier than a Pinto, four-speed versus four-speed. However, Chevrolet's problems went deeper. The linerless bore, alloy block Chevy four had big NVH issues. The 2.3's reliability woes outweighed its alloy weight saving. In addition, the Vega's optional automatic gearbox was the two-speed Powerglide unit. That didn't bode well for good performance or economy.

Speaking of initial impressions, Pinto made a good one with *Super Stock and Drag Illustrated* magazine. The journal tested a 2-liter coupe in December 1970. it was impressed in an overall

This 1976 Pinto Runabout MPG survivor has only 7254 miles on the odometer, and is part of a private collection. After the recessionary effects of the first gas crunch, Pinto sales recovered in 1976 to nearly 300,000 units. (Courtesy www.duncanimports.com)

In the wake of the first fuel crisis, Ford advertising claimed the new '75 Ford Pinto MPG, at 34mpg and $2769, had better gas mileage at a lower price than the leading foreign import. (Courtesy www.duncanimports.com)

sense concerning Pinto, and felt fit and finish were superior to chief rival Vega. Although, in light of the Chevy's shortcomings, the phrase 'shooting fish in a barrel' comes to mind. *Road & Track* also had reservations concerning Pinto's handling and standard four-wheel drums. Just okay for urban use, but with Pinto the optional front disk brakes were strongly recommended. It spoke to Detroit's attitude towards economy cars being low cost and basic. Pinto's disk/drum set-up involved 9.3in front disks and 9 x 1.4in rear drums.

In November 1971 *Car and Driver* considered the $50 2-liter motor and $32 front disk brakes to be bargain Pinto options. The magazine also echoed *R&T*'s sentiment concerning handling. In praise *C/D* said: "The Pinto is exceptionally satisfying as a city traffic car." It was acknowledged that Pinto was maneuverable, had good visibility and was agile like a sports car. However, as a highway car, the subcompact's lack of directional stability and harsh ride were a problem.[6]

Accessory groups

The Pinto Rallye Appearance Group consisted of blackout grille with Rallye Badge, black taillamp bezels, black or gold hood center, black rear valence with periphery molding. From the Accent Group: chrome B-pillar, drip moldings, window frames, wheel lip moldings and color-keyed carpets, driver-side remote control/color-keyed racing mirror. Boss

Mustang-style side decal stripe, bright tailpipe trim piece, chrome hubcaps/trim rings, A 78-13 BSW tires, manual front disk brakes. Interior sports shift knob, shift pattern diagram on shifter boot, chrome parking brake handle with simulation wood grip.

To boost their bottom line, dealers were hoping buyers would specify Pinto's accessory groups. The Accent Group also had deluxe chrome wheelcovers which were also in the Luxury Décor Group. This exterior/interior pack included all Accent Group stuff, plus rocker panel chrome molding and upscale interior. One could also get a fashionable vinyl roof! The dealers and buyers were happy. Captive imports didn't have the range and type of visual and creature features that domestic buyers wanted. Hence the need for Henry's own American small economy and sporty duo: Pinto & Mustang II. Only a domestic could provide a vinyl roof and V6 or V8 option!

Total performance & economy

As true as it has always been, the first thing most consumers look at is price. In March and April 1967, when *Motor Trend* was observing the small car market, it remarked on 2 grand being a psychological barrier in the minds of economy car buyers. This was so at the time the Pinto project started, and was still the case at launch. Henry's subcompact made an $1850 debut. This was noticeably under Chevy Vega. FoMoCo never had a car this cheap,

With fuel miser packages in vogue, Ford made value comparisons with the Chevy Chevette Scooter. The ads advanced the line that a four-seater Pinto MPG with 92bhp made more good horse sense than a two-seater Scooter with 52bhp. Sometimes you're going to need that back seat! (Courtesy www.duncanimports.com)

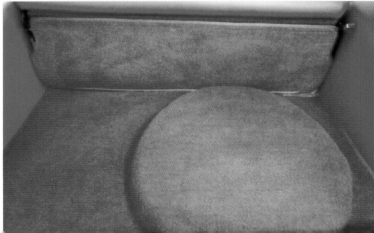

since its 1958 six-cylinder-powered standard family car. January 1971 saw AMC Gremlin on $1879 and fully imported Beetle at $1880.

Even *Car and Driver* remarked how the Pinto undercut the high-tech Vega substantially. By later in 1971, this entry point for a two-door sedan had climbed to $1919, but Vega was on $2197 by this stage. However, all the above were window sticker showroom bait prices, for basic cars no one would really buy by choice. Dealers didn't like to stock such low profit margin rides either. The path to happiness lies with optioning. Sensibly so for Pinto that would be the $130 Luxury Décor Group, $61 AM radio, $29 fold out rear windows, $36 fold-down rear seat and $87 A70-13 tires. And now, it even cost money to save money.

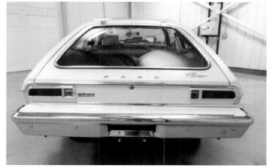

As part of the Pinto's economy car raison d'etre, Ford sold a beginner's tool kit costing $29, master toolkit for $45 and associated instruction manual for a couple of bucks. With all this an owner was supposed to be able to reduce overall ownership costs by doing some, or all service work themselves. Experience with such apparatus, which included a

In America's Bicentennial year of 1976, FoMoCo was doing what many said couldn't be done: profitably make a volume-produced, American-designed small car, in the USA. (Courtesy www.duncanimports.com)

The '70s brought a new phenomenon: the expensive economy car. People were spending more to save money. (Courtesy Ford Motor Co)

multi-purpose Swiss Army knife style tool, was mixed. *Car and Driver*'s 15,000 mile November '71 report saw them in favor of the kit. Having discovered a poor level of service from various Ford dealers, it said the self service manual and kits were easy to follow and use.

Consumer Reports' January 1971 report took a negative view concerning the usefulness of the 'U-Service Kit.' For a start, the all-purpose FoMoCo tool that was a screwdriver, ruler, feeler gauge and sparkplug gapping tool, didn't work too well. Even when

This 1978 Pinto Country Squire wagon has the optional 2.8-liter Cologne V6, and dual color-keyed side reversing mirrors. The C3 Cruise-O-Matic autobox was a commonly chosen option. (Courtesy www.duncanimports.com)

turning to its CU workshop equipment, the journal couldn't get their '71 Pinto to run properly using the instruction manual's advice. It gave the car to Ford, whose own technicians bypassed the fuel mixture and ignition timing settings writtens so that the car could function normally. There is no doubt federal smog regulations were playing merry hell, concerning getting an early '70s car to start, idle and run properly. This was so even with the car warmed up, unless it had fuel-injection. *Car and Driver* had its own workshop facilities as well. It didn't state whether it had utilized the Ford multi-purpose tool.

The idea of buying a kit to service an inexpensive car seemed like a very old-fashioned *Leave It to Beaver*, Mobil Economy Run era view of economy car ownership. The early '70s small car buyer in America wanted a reliable, well-finished machine, no bigger than his or her intended driving purposes required. However, they surely didn't wish to carry out their own maintenance work? That wasn't part of the no muss, no fuss VW or Japanese small car experience. The cynical might venture that such self-service kits were an attempt to make a few more bucks out of a prospect, before they drove off.

Servicing was a side issue; did Pinto better Beetle in the value for money economy car stakes? In price, comfort and acceleration, plus practicality, it

would have to be an objective yes. The front-engined, quasi-hatchback format was much more livable and useful than a rear-engined small car. *Consumer Reports*' 1978lb Super Beetle cost $2139 and did 0-60mph in 20 seconds. The also four-speed Pinto 2-liter could halve that time, providing a welcome safety margin over the 1600cc Bug. And the Bug's marginal performance allowed it to only match the thrifty Pinto's overall gas mileage. That's Henry one, Dr Porsche zero!

The Super Beetle's new MacPherson strut front suspension was something pioneered by FoMoCo on popular cars. Intended to boost ride comfort and trunk capacity versus Pinto and modern rivals. However, *Consumer Reports* found it did neither. It seemed like small cars were borrowing from Ford. Saab turned to Ford Germany for its V4 motor. Much more powerful and practical than that old two-stroke. The Simca's door key was reversible for convenience – a Ford trick. However, there seemed one lesson from old Europe that Pinto had yet to learn: quality control. New designs do have teething problems in design and execution for the buyer. They are understandable, but annoying.

The Super Beetle recorded a record low number of defects found on the car: just 11. So it was even better built than the Datsun and Toyota. It also had the best warranty: two years or 24,000

This 1978 Pinto Country Squire has only 51,000 miles on the clock. By 1976, the VW Super Beetle was impersonating Detroit plushness with La Grande Bug. But interior packaging and weight-saving, meant the Ford Escort and VW Rabbit went front drive with transverse motor. (Courtesy www.duncanimports.com)

miles. These two facts explained the Bug's great resale value: another aspect of cost in terms of depreciation saved. The Ford Pinto tested had the greatest number of delivered defects at 30. In overall test results, *Consumer Reports* gave Datsun 1st place, Vega came 2nd and Toyota 3rd. This was a judgment on new cars. It is known that in terms of body corrosion and engine trouble, Vega provided more headaches than other small cars.[7]

It wasn't a recall item, but many 2-liter Pintos built in the fall of 1970 had their cams installed ten degrees out of phase. This mistake caused poor drivability. Ford did send a Tech Service Bulletin to dealers, but many Ford mechanics weren't told about it. As for early recalls, there were a

few. On October 30 1970, 26,000 Pintos were recalled due to gas pedals sticking at over halfway travel. On March 29 1971, 220,000 Pintos made prior to March 19 1971 were recalled due to air fuel vapors possibly igniting from an engine backfire. Not as bad as Vega – not even close – but annoying.

True, the three domestic subcompacts were new designs, but lessons were obviously learned by Ford. The Mustang II had a solid reputation for quality from the get go. However, that ride was an upscale, mini personal coupe. The irony was that the sticking throttle problem was on the reliable Kent–powered Pintos. Even so, quality snafus didn't prevent Pinto from being a sales winner. In spite of Gremlins getting in early, and mighty Chevrolet as a rival, Ford's Pinto reached a '71 MY total of 352,402. And this was in the Beetle's final worldwide million-selling year.

Pinto production took place at Edison Assembly in New Jersey, San Jose Assembly in California, and St Thomas Assembly in Ontario, Canada. There were more model variants than just the two-door sedan: this variant ended its run at the close of '72 MY. The important three-door hatchback, dubbed Runabout, made its debut at the Chicago Auto Show. Runabout was on sale from February 20 1971, at a price of $2062. The extra money provided mechanical chrome hinges, five decorative roof chrome strips, pneumatic hatch struts, and a fold-down rear seat. Henry Ford II had a '71 Runabout himself. The hatchback version ran until Pinto's 1980 demise.

On February 24 1972, the Pinto wagon version became available. In the pre impact bumper era it measured 172.7in long, and offered a very commodious 60.5ft^3 of cargo space. It was the first two-door Ford wagon since 1961, and with SoCal surfer culture, could lay claim to being an early lifestyle vehicle. Pinto wagon brought standard flip-open rear ¼ windows, front disk brakes, rear HD drums, and the 2-liter OHC motor. In Ford tradition, the Pinto

Pesky pollution controls sapped engine power. So the Kent 1.6 and EAO 2-liter I4s were history at the end of '73 and '74 MYs respectively. The Lima 2.3 I4 became the new base motor in 1975. It was joined at the same time by the optional Cologne V6 shown. (Courtesy www.duncanimports.com)

Country Squire was an upscale edition with exterior faux wood paneling. Pinto cruised to a 480,405 '72 MY sales total.

Ford's predilection for a myriad of model iterations prompted *Car and Driver* to wonder what of the Pinto GT, Brougham, Country Squire, Sports Roof and Pinto Cobra? The journal's September 1970 wishes would eventually be granted. They rightly assumed Henry was working on getting the starter two-door sedan right, before moving on to diversity, like Pinto Rallye. This accessory package-cum-youth variant answered the call for subcompact insurance premium fighting sporty cars. Pinto Rallye with 2-liter motor and four-speed really delivered on the paint and tape promise.

With insurance companies getting heavy with even small block compacts, like Maverick Grabber 302 and Chevy Nova SS 350, the youth vote was swinging to AMC Gremlin X 258 and sporty Vegas. Although Vega Cosworth was a different upscale kettle of fish, some years away. Pinto was named after the pony with distinctive white and solid color patches. 2-liter '71 Pinto Rallye four-speed had enough ponies to outpace VW Sports Bug, Vega with optional 110bhp motor, and even Gremlin X 258! *Car and Driver*'s figures showed a well run in 2-liter Pinto four-speed could hit sixty in 10.5 seconds, and complete a ¼ mile in 17.6 seconds at 76mph. It hit 80mph in exactly

With a 60.5ft³ cargo capacity, Ford's Pinto wagon offered a practical alternative for those wishing to downsize from midsize wagons. Its 172.7in pre-impact bumper length made Pinto wagon sensibly sized. (Courtesy www.duncanimports.com)

The Pinto wagon's extra length meant it wasn't caught up in the NHTSA fire safety recall of 1978. The wagon variant also proved an invaluable addition to the custom van scene. (Courtesy www.duncanimports.com)

20 seconds, and was a genuine 100mph machine. Hi ho 'lil pony!

In the enthusiast area, Pinto got the smooth revving 2.8-liter Cologne V6 as a 1975 option. The Gremlin had been stealing sales from Pinto and Vega for years, due to AMC offering the only subcompact with a big six. The 2.8-liter V6 wasn't as punchy as AMC's 4.2 motor, but it was more than Chevy had, except for that pricey Cosworth. The Cologne V6 was a smooth, rev happy device. That said, dealers oftentimes didn't stock Pinto V6s. The same went for Pinto's upscale cousin, the Mercury Bobcat. Figuring that subcompacts and inline fours went together like lox and cream cheese, Pinto and Bobcat V6s were always rarer. Dare it be said, those looking for fancily trimmed Vee-powered subcompacts took the Mustang II and Chevy Monza route.

In an attempt to cover all bases, and have something upscale for the 'lil lady of a Lincoln-Mercury patron, the badge-engineered Bobcat joined the luxo car dealer chain, once the Pantera had said arrivederci. The Bobcat and Pinto were very similar, aside from detail front grille alterations and nicer standard Mercury interior trim. Bobcat availability commenced a year earlier in Canada, for 1974 model year. The Bobcat continued

until Pinto left the building in 1980. There was even an accompanying wagon version that went by the moniker Bobcat Villager. All in all, 224,026 Bobcats were built. It was available with the same bodystyles and engine options as the same era of Pinto. Like Pinto, the wagon variant continued until the discontinuation of the Bobcat range.

Over time Ford's engineers tried boosting the practicality of Pinto hatchback. The fold-down rear seat had increased luggage capacity to 38.1ft^3. However, there was the issue of accessing this area, and vehicle looks. To improve both for '72 MY, the hatch glass was enlarged to almost liftback size. Next step was a full glass hatch. This looked great and was also available on Bobcat. However, for the ultimate lifestyle subcompact on the planet, one couldn't go past the 1977 Ford Pinto Cruising

Pinto's North American production took place at Edison Assembly (New Jersey), San Jose Assembly (California), and St Thomas Assembly (Ontario). This plate shows the Pinto was made in America in 1978, the handbook showing a major anniversary for Ford America, however, in the future their business would be much different. It is known that come the '80s and beyond there would be use of 'back door' imports and Mexican production,to get around cost issues. (Courtesy www.duncanimports.com)

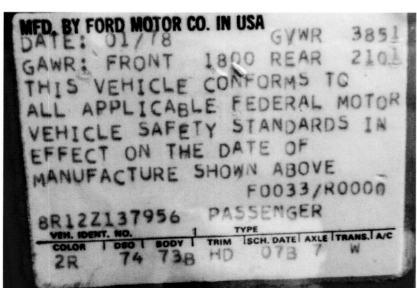

Wagon package. The Cruising wagon was based on the Pinto sedan delivery variant. With a nod to the late '70s custom van scene, this van conversion came with vacuum-formed porthole bubble side windows. It was natural for the era; if it wasn't round you really were square. Fantabulous side graphics, and FoMoCo's 13 x 5in steel sport rims made Pinto Cruising Wagon a genuine factory-fresh custom ride! Well, Ford was ahead of the curve on that score. The 1977 Pinto Cruising Wagon had a like-liveried companion … the Cruising Van!

The same style side stripes, porthole bubble window and custom interior applied to both. However, the van received full shagpile carpeting – another decorative mainstay of the era. Whether it was the TV home den, or custom van love den, it just had to have that full shag treatment. Exterior paint and stripe color combos was myriad. Just consult your local Ford dealer for a brochure. In 1964, Ford was first with a dealer-supplied turn-key drag racer called Thunderbolt. Now, in disco times, Henry had done it again … with customized van and wagon!

Like the Ford ad said, Dearborn took all the hard work out of customization. Both 'Cruising' rides looked like you paid a talented guy in Van Nuys a small fortune, and commissioned Von Dutch to do the graphics. For the Pinto Cruising Wagon Ford said: "Part wagon, part van, all fun." A little corny, but true, and it came with a front spoiler, dual racing mirrors, trim rings and Rallye Pack. Van and wagon also came with the lower third blackout treatment, for a sleeker look.

Federal trials & tribulations
In 1972 Ford came up with the Sprint Décor Option, to celebrate the coming summer '72 Munich Olympics. It was available on Pinto, Maverick and Mustang. For Pinto Runabout that meant red, white and blue exterior accents, trim rings and color-keyed hubcaps, dual racing mirrors, red, white and blue cloth and vinyl buckets, deluxe two-spoke steering wheel, full carpeting, rear ¼ panel Stars & Stripes decal, A78 x 13 white sidewall tires, and blackout grille. However, there was one item missing: Pinto's optional 100 horse 2.0-liter SOHC I4.

Sadly, the industry-wide compression ratio drop had reduced the Kent and EAO 2.0 to 54 and 86 net horses respectively for 1972. Blame GM and those draconian feds! The latter wanted tightened emissions, the former used its lobby group muscle to make a CR drop the method of choice. During '71 MY, Ford had advanced timing from six to ten degrees BTDC, revised carb settings and introduced hotter sparkplugs with a wider gap. This was all done with the stricter '72 MY emissions requirements in mind. This was then combined with the CR drop.

1978 was the last year Pinto shared its styling with the already defunct Maverick. Ford's successful front drive Euro Ford Fiesta captive import of 1978-80 ate into Pinto small car sales. (Courtesy Country Classic Cars countryclassiccars.com)

In the '70s, the 2.3-liter I4 Pinto and Vega were considered small. However, for the '80s, designers downsized further in the wake of the 2nd gas crunch. Now it was all 1.6-liter front drive hatches, like the Ford Escort. (Courtesy Country Classic Cars countryclassiccars.com)

It just wasn't the same underhood anymore. Come 1974 and the Kent was gone, the 2-liter was Pinto's new base motor, and the 2.3 Lima I4 was optional. Pollution controls were taking their toll. In 1974, *Car and Driver* sampled a Pinto with C3 automatic, and noted that the autobox made gas mileage and acceleration appreciably worse.

With the arrival of the 1973/74 fuel crisis, and very tightened emissions regs for 1975, the Lima 2300 became the base motor for '75 MY. 1974 had seen the Pinto re-bumpered to be federally compliant with 5mph impacts. 1975 also saw the MPG spec arrive to save gas; it was soon shared with the Mustang II as well. It was a busy time, so a '75 base Pinto was now a four-speed stick 2580lb subcompact, measuring 169in long. It had a 13 gallon gas tank and 3.18 rear axle. Not the 'gas hog' 3.55:1 anymore!

Its Lima 2.3 I4 had an 8.4:1 CR and Motorcraft two-barrel carb. It all equaled 83bhp at 4800rpm and 109lb/ft at 2800rpm. Concerning maneuverability, Pinto's turning circle was 30.7ft. The Mercury Bobcat V6 version had the same size tank. With C3 automatic it weighed 2755lb, and its Cologne V6 made 97bhp at 4400rpm and 138lb/ft at 3200rpm.[8] The Bobcat also had a 3.18 rear axle, and 4.2 turns lock to lock for its manual steering. Both also came with BR78-13 tires.

For budget high performance fans, the 2.3 Lima's long production run saw useful off the shelf hardware offered over the years. Of the various 2.3-liter cylinder heads, the D-port open chamber type flows best. The oval port can make good power with porting and polishing. These heads are cheap and plentiful. Round port Ford Ranger heads flow okay, but are harder to find a sports intake manifold for to suit. The late model Ford Ranger exhaust manifold, Ford part number F57Z-9430-C, is almost like a performance header set-up.

The Lima motor can be bored out for more displacement. As much as 0.040in, with the overbore done in instalments, 0.030in first, then 0.010in. There was a time when the Cologne V6 and 302 V8 conversions, were the engine swaps of choice for Pinto. However, great power and better weight distribution, has seen the turbo Lima 2.3 I4, with over 200bhp from the factory alone, take over in modification popularity. The Pinto underwent some structural and hardware changes over the years. Early cars, 1970-73, were 200lb lighter with thinner sheetmetal, but still not as thin as Vega! These Pintos had fewer sheetmetal reinforcements. Front suspension spindle height, upper and lower A-arms and the steering rack were all different. 1974 also saw front disk brakes become standard equipment. The production changes are key for circle track racing, and were noted by Steve Smith in his February 2009 article for *Circle Track* magazine.

USA

Ford

Ford Division, Ford Motor Co.,
300 Renaissance Center, Detroit, Michigan 48243, USA

As Ford headed towards the World Car, the Pinto and Bobcat ranges were restyled for 1979 to match the new Fairmont/Foxstang look. The Pinto Cruising Wagon continued as a factory exponent of the custom car scene. (Courtesy Vereinigte Motor-Verlage)

Ford Mustang Cobra 97 kW, 195 km/h

Ford Pinto 66–76 kW, 150–165 km/h

Ford Pinto Cruising Wagon 66–76 kW, 150–165 km/h

Ford Granada 72–102 kW, 150–160 km/h

Ford Fairmont 66–104 kW, 150–180 km/h

Unter den amerikanischen Autoherstellern bleibt Ford als Nr. 2 fest im Sattel. Das Firmenangebot besteht nach wie vor aus drei Marken einschließlich des Firmen-(und Familien-)namens. Die Marke Ford stellt das Fundament des Angebots dar, mit Modellen vom kompakten Pinto bis zum nicht mehr ganz so großen LTD. Die Mercurys sind Modell für Modell von den Fords abgeleitet und im wesentlichen identisch. Die Lincolns, auch technisch eng mit den größeren Fords verwandt, sind die Prestige-Marke. Alle Modelle konventioneller Bauart.

Ford Pinto
Seit 1970 gebauter Kompaktwagen mit neuen Stylingdetails, Aluminium-Stoßstangen, neuen Ausstattungspaketen 2,3 Liter-Vierzylinder, 2,8 Liter-V6 aus „Old Germany" stehen zur Wahl; zweitürige Limou-

sine, Kombicoupé und Kombiwagen—verkaufen sich wieder gut bei der jetzigen Benzinknappheit. Ab $ 3233.

Ford Mustang
Ein im wesentlichen neues Auto; zugleich größer, geräumiger, jedoch leichter als sein Vorgänger. Basiert auf dem vor zwei Jahren vorgestellten Ford Fairmont. In der Mustang-Tradition bleibt das neue Modell ein 2+2-Sitzer mit sportlichem Charakter. Breite Motorenpalette: der 2,3 Liter-Vierzylinder in Saug- und Turboversionen, der deutsche 2,8-V6, seit Anfang 1979 der bekannte 3,3 Liter-Reihensechszylinder (beide Motoren nur mit Automatik) und der 4,9 Liter-V8. Letzterer mit dem Viergang-Overdrive-Getriebe ist merkwürdig „langbeinig", denn der Motor dreht bei 100 km/h nur etwa 2000/min. Michelin TRX-Reifen gegen Aufpreis erhältlich, im Zusammenhang mit einem Handling-Paket. Ab $ 4187.

Ford Fairmont/Futura
In seinem ersten Produktionsjahr verkaufte sich der Fairmont besser als jedes andere US-Modell in der Geschichte des Autos. Die Angebotspalette ist nunmehr erweitert worden. Das Viergang-Getriebe (Overdrive wie beim Mustang) hat ein Dreigang-Getriebe als Standardausrüstung mit dem 3,3 Liter-Reihensechszylinder ersetzt und ist auch mit dem V8-Motor erhältlich, wogegen der Achtzylinder früher nur mit Automatik zu haben war. Basismotor bleibt der 2,3 Liter-Vierzylinder. Wie beim Mustang McPherson-Vorderradaufhängung, starre Hinterachse an Längs- und Schräglenkern mit Schraubenfedern. Ab $ 3770.

Ford Granada
Mit den sich rapide ändernden Verhältnissen in Amerika

The Pinto's front suspension, and Lincoln Versailles' 9in rear axle with disk brakes were utilized for '30s and '40s hot rods before the aftermarket accommodated such needs. (Courtesy Vereinigte Motor-Verlage)

Lincoln

Lincoln-Mercury Division, Ford Motor Co.,
300 Renaissance Center, Detroit, Michigan 48243, USA

Lincoln Versailles   97 kW, 155 km/h

Lincoln Continental   119 kW, 170 km/h

Lincoln Continental Mark V   119 kW, 175 km/h

Neben Cadillac bleibt der Lincoln die Prestigemarke auf dem amerikanischen Markt. Interessant dabei ist, daß der ehemalige Cadillac-Präsident Leland 1917 die Firma Lincoln gründete, die dann fünf Jahre später von Ford erworben wurde. Der Lincoln Continental als Top-modell ist der Dienstwagen des US-Präsidenten.

Lincoln Versailles
Leicht modifizierte Version des Ford Granada, aber die äußerliche Identität des Versailles wurde für den jetzigen Jahrgang durch ein neues Dachhinterteil betont. Neu auch sind Halogenscheinwerfer, die gemäß einem neuen Gesetz die doppelte Beleuchtungsstärke leisten, und ein vollelektronisches Quadrosonic-Radio. Vierrad-Scheibenbremsen, Automatik, Servolenkung, automatische Klimaanlage, Cassettenspieler serienmäßig. Ab $ 13 206.

Lincoln Continental
„Letzter der Dinosaurier." Dieser riesige Familienwagen, als Limousine und Coupé angeboten, war der letzte ungeschwächte amerikanische Big Car und verkaufte sich noch im vorletzten Produktionsjahr sehr rege: mehr als 93 000 davon! Dann im Juni 1979, als die Bevölkerung in Benzinschlangen wartete, wurde die Produktion eingestellt. Neue, abgemagerte Modelle erscheinen im Herbst 1979. Preis für die letzten Exemplare: ab $ 11 252.

Continental Mark V
Auch mit diesem Riesencoupé geht eine Ära zu Ende. 5,85 Meter lang, 2,13 Tonnen schwer, 6,6 Liter V8-Motor. Die Collector's Series feiert sein letztes Jahr in „fullsize", die Designer Series bietet noch immer Versionen von Bill Blass, Emilio Pucci, Givenchy und Cartier. Preise ab $ 13 334.

Mercury

Lincoln-Mercury Division, Ford Motor Co.,
300 Renaissance Center, Detroit, Michigan 48243, USA

Mercury Bobcat   66–76 kW, 150–165 km/h

Mercurys sechs Modellreihen, im wesentlichen mit entsprechenden Ford-Modellen identisch, weisen im jetzigen Jahrgang zwei Neuheiten auf: den Capri und die großen Marquis/Grand Marquis.

Mercury Bobcat
Mercury-Version des Ford Pinto; nur als dreitüriges Kombicoupé und Kombi erhältlich. In seiner aktuellsten Fassung weist der Bobcat ähnliche Änderungen wie sein

Ford-Zwillingsbruder auf: neue Frontpartie, Stoßstangen und Interieur-Details, verbesserte Leistung beim V6-Motor. Neue Extras: MW-UKW-Stereo-Radio mit Cassettenspieler, Leichtmetallräder. Ab $ 3797.

Mercury Capri
Seit Anfang August 1978 wird der europäische Ford Capri nicht mehr nach den USA exportiert. An seine Stelle trat Ende 1978 ein neuer, in Ame-

STOCK VERSION

MOLDED IN SILVER

FOR AGES 10 TO ADULT
PHOTOS OF PAINTED PROTOTYPE MODEL

PINTO **Pony** EXPRESS

STREET MACHINE VERSION

1/25 SCALE MODEL KIT / MODELE REDUIT

mpc®

Pinto – a subcompact to remember

Pinto hit its best sales figures in 1974, 544,209 were sold. In 1976 it fell back to 290,132 units. However, for the rest of the 1975-80 period it was around 200,000 units. Small car competition was heating up. There was the new VW Rabbit, Chevy Chevette, Mazda GLC and other Japanese imports … Renault LeCar, anyone? Then there was the successful Dodge Colt captive import. Suffice to say things were getting crowded. Plus, the definition of a small car was getting smaller. Even the AMC Gremlin went to a four-cylinder option. There was also much talk of the World Car. A front drive, transverse-engined four-cylinder hatchback, with design input from around the world, but also one design

that could be sold all over the world, with minimal changes. That's the car Pinto's replacement would be. The 1981 Ford Escort had a connection with the next generation Mazda GLC. Mazda was Ford's small car partner. Strange bedfellows does a fuel crisis make.

The Escort was the first car PBS show *MotorWeek* tested. Before that, the Pinto and Bobcat were made over, with front fascia restyling to match the new Fairmont/Mustang look. The Maverick had parted company in 1977, and used to be the Pinto's styling inspiration. In spite of all the controversy, and persistent criticisms of Ford and Detroit in general, the Pinto had been a successful car. A sales tally of 3173,491, mainly from one country, is quite something. For 1980 the V6 option was gone, and final ads asked

With its Cruising Van and like-liveried Pinto Cruising Wagon, Ford had created the first factory turn key, showroom-ready custom vehicles. However, that didn't stop enthusiasts taking things a step further! (Courtesy round2corp.com)

Americans to "Rallye Around The 1980 Pinto." A clever patriotic play on the Rallye package and flag.

In some ways stemming the small car import tide had been a losing battle. Whenever Detroit introduced a new small car line, it was feared the automaker would just cannibalize sales from its larger line, rather than get conquest sales from the imports. For example, Maverick ate into Mustang sales more than the VW Beetle. Similarly, Pinto dented Maverick sales. Ford eventually returned to captive imports in 1978 with the Fiesta. It was the first front drive Ford sold in the U.S.A. This new sub Rabbit-sized car, once again using ye olde Kent I4, was a product of Ford Europe. Unfortunately CAFE would soon rule out captive imports from contributing to the fleet average. So Henry needed a small American car of his own, once again. If you can't beat 'em, join 'em. That's where small car partner Mazda came in, and that's where Ford was heading.

For a decade, the Pinto was Ford's subcompact import fighter. It garnered 3,173,491 sales and a fair amount of controversy. The latter was largely unwarranted. (Courtesy City View Classic Cars – Texas)

Drag racing

The Pinto hit the strip very early on with 2-liter power, thanks to Bill Neumann. Neumann, a pioneer in the four-cylinder sport compact business, could see potential in the Pinto. Neumann was originally an East Coast hot rodder. At the time of the '71 MY Pinto, he had an agency and clients including Isky Cams, Offenhauser, and Arias Pistons. Neumann felt a hot four-cylinder American subcompact could provide a new business avenue for such firms.

Bill Neumann had contacts at Ford. He put together a prototype ¼ mile improved Pinto 2-liter four-speed, with its build-up covered in a series of *Popular Hot Rodding* magazine articles. Readers were really turned on by the sight of a 14 second Pinto wearing slot mags. The mini machine registered 98 rear wheel horsepower and a 14.56 second ET at 91.33mph. Better than an early 2000s SVT Focus!

Neumann received many enquiries, and the Neumann Distributing business of mail order performance parts supply quickly overtook the ad agency work. Bill Neumann then went on to Datsun 510s and 240Zs. As with the Pinto, such overhead cam small cars could be tuned to give V8 performance, while retaining super gas mileage. Eventually he set up the Neuspeed brand, specializing in German and Asian imports. However, it all started with Henry's subcompact![9]

In the late '60s, road circuit racing in the form of the SCCA's Trans Am series and NASCAR took on major national interest. The former tied in nicely with the pony car's zenith, as sports fans saw their heroes drive cars that looked like what lived in their garage. NASCAR had the Mopar versus Ford Aero Wars, updated circuits and the billing as the racing sport of choice for the '70s.

However, both areas of racing kinda deflated by the early '70s. Public – and

The triumphant Gapp & Roush Pinto that Wayne Gapp raced to the 1973 NHRA Pro Stock title. In doing so, Gapp set a P/S record ET of 8.89 seconds. (Courtesy Roush Automotive Collection)

the big three manufacturer – interest decreased. There just wasn't that much cash around. Drag racing wasn't immune from the 1970's economic woes, but regional and national interest kept going. This was especially so with the NHRA's Pro Stock category. The authority's rulebook changes were in favor of small-block V8 subcompacts, like Ford Pinto and Mustang II.

The drag racing team of chassis guru Wayne Gapp and Cactus Jack Roush started in 1971. Racer Wayne Gapp was Ford's drag racing program principal engineer. Unfortunately, he also had a private racing business. One day Ford said there was a conflict of interest, and he had to choose between the two. No problem; in stepped former Ford employee Jack Roush. Roush then ran Gapp's racing outfit.

The Michigan duo became famous for their 427 SOHC-powered Maverick, called the Tijuana Taxi. However, the NHRA were opening the door to small-block powered subcompacts in Pro Stock, to break that Mopar Hemi dominance. It all meant Pinto time for Gapp & Roush. Their first foray with Ford's Pinto in 1972 wasn't too successful. They sold this little

number to Bob Glidden, who did have some success with Pinto. Indeed, Gapp & Roush provided knowledge and support for Pinto Pro Stock racers, concerning Glidden and Barrie Poole. Meanwhile, Gapp & Roush had found Pinto success with a new Pinto of their own.

Gapp & Roush had a new chassis design 1973 racing season Pinto ready to go, and this time their little subcompact was a winner. Except for the Pro Stock final of the 1973 NHRA Gatornationals. Here, Dyno Don Nicholson's Pinto just beat out the Gapp & Roush Pinto driven by Wayne Gapp. However, that year Gapp & Roush won the 1973 NHRA World Finals, and set a new national record in the process. Their Pinto Pro Stock record was an 8.89 second pass. The duo were also somewhat following Dyno Don's lead, by starting to campaign a Pro Stock Mustang II in 1974.

With success came diversification. As a busy outfit, Gapp & Roush fielded as many as three cars on the Pro Stock circuit. One was driven by Ken Dondero. In addition, match racing is very different to national event drag racing. With a view to getting into match racing action, Gapp & Roush bought Barrie

By the early '70s, small-block, V8-powered subcompacts had come to the Pro Stock fore, thanks to NHRA rule changes concerning weight breaks. Jack Roush eventually had an accident that wrecked this G&R Pinto. (Courtesy Roush Automotive Collection)

Poole's Pinto. Poole had experienced a bad snowmobile accident, and Gapp & Roush got this ex Poole/Elliot Pinto to tackle match races. Unfortunately for their fans, the Gapp & Roush partnership ended in 1975. Jack Roush was tempted by NASCAR, going that route in 1976. Wayne Gapp continued to work for Ford, and retired from drag racing in 1978. Jack Roush's Blue Oval connection continues to the present.

Dyno Don Nicholson had success in Pro Stock with the Ford Pinto too. Dyno Don had made his way back to this racing format, by converting Jerry Harvey's 1966 A/FX Mustang to P/S configuration. He won the street class in A/Modified Production at the 1969 Springnationals. A SOHC 427 Maverick was followed by a number of P/S Fords. Noting the popularity of Super Stocks, the NHRA used the Pro Stock name for their sanctioned races from 1970.

After his winning Maverick, Dyno Don went to a '72 P/S 351C Pinto. At the start of the 1973 season, he won three consecutive national events. The Cleveland-powered Pinto won the

AHRA Winternationals, NHRA Winternationals and NHRA Gatornationals. A great Pro Stock springboard to his next winning machine, the P/S Mustang II.

At the start of the 1973 racing season, Dyno Don's 351C-powered P/S Pinto won three consecutive national events. (Courtesy round2corp.com)

Dyno Don's successful '73 racing season P/S Pinto at the 2006 Englehart Performance Show. (Courtesy Chris)

Dyno Don Nicholson was an early bird on the Pro Stock scene. He recognised the potential popularity of the format, and ran a succession of P/S small-block Fords. (Courtesy Bill Crittenden www. carsandracingstuff.com)

Bob Glidden's Pinto was the most successful Pro Stock racer of its era. Glidden drove the car to three NHRA Pro Stock World Championship titles, and twenty NHRA national event victories. (Courtesy www.mecum.com)

The most successful Pro Stock Pinto racer was Bob Glidden. His car won three NHRA Pro Stock World Championships. He edged out Wayne Gapp's Gapp & Roush Mustang II in 1974, winning the title again in 1975 and 1978 with the same Pinto. This Pinto won twenty NHRA national events, and combined with the three World titles, made this car the winningest Pro Stocker of its era. In 1974 it won the Springnationals, US Nationals and set a national record of an 8.83 second pass at 154.90mph.

The Glidden Pinto featured a chrome moly tube frame, and 351C/5-speed powertrain. The 377 cube Cleveland was a custom job by Glidden, featuring many special design or modified parts. The oil lubrication system, pistons, rods, crank, valvetrain, heads, fuel supply and ignition were all modified. So was the intake manifold design. There were few gages in the fiberglass dashboard, to monitor the 650bhp Boss motor. The V8 exhaled through special Hooker headers. Hooker was allowed to use this Pinto as a test

Glidden's Pinto used a 377ci version of FoMoCo's 351 Cleveland V8, but with many custom touches. It made 650 horses, was connected to a five-speed, and exhaled through Hooker headers. (Courtesy www.mecum.com)

mule for its Pro Stock racing program hardware R&D. The Glidden Pinto featured the work of Hooker's engineers.

Bob Glidden's Pinto was originally painted red. It then famously featured Stars & Stripes livery courtesy of Glidden's partner, Bob Allen, during the 1975 and 1976 racing seasons. It was the only race car Glidden ever sold complete with its power team. Oftentimes when racing outfits sell their cars, they retain the engine and gearbox.

Road circuit racing

Back when road circuit cars weren't far removed from showroom machines, and manufacturers sweetened the sponsor pot and created homologation specials and parts, the Trans Am series ruled. There were two categories, under two liters and under five liters. American pony cars took care of the V8 area, Alfa Romeo, Porsche and BMW did the former. The 5-liter category imploded at the close of 1970. There was less buyer interest in pony cars, and hence manufacturers were less willing to fund racing.

To maintain interest in Trans Am road circuit racing, the smaller engine class was up limited to 2.5-liters, creating the SCCA 2-5 (Two-Five) Challenge Series. The move brought a more diverse group of cars, including domestic machines. One example was the Galpin Ford dealer sponsored Ford Pinto. Galpin Ford sold Pintos in Southern California, so why

not race them and get more publicity? The large dealer has a stellar history in motorsport and vehicle modification. In the Pinto's era it was still under the control of Bert Boeckmann. The car it campaigned had an I4 stroked to 2.5 liters, and fed by huge Weber 48 DCOE sidedraft carbs. It was set up to live in the 5500 to 9000rpm zone.

The 2-5 Challenge lost its way during 1972, when the Datsun 510 became super dominant. Even after the SCCA canned the 2-5 Challenge, the Galpin Pinto continued to compete. It eventually did vintage race events up to 2010. Not long after this, the Galpin Auto Sports (GAS) collection learned of the car's existence. It added the special Pinto to its collection, fixing it, but not restoring it. As if by a miracle, it has survived in very neat, well-preserved condition … with original paint!

The Pinto, like the SCCA itself, didn't have such an easy time with the 2-5 Challenge for small cars. Ford's subcompact found more success in the equivalent B F Goodrich Radial Challenge, offered by IMSA. Once again, it was a road circuit racing series for grocery getters. Six-cylinder Gremlins and Hornets featured, but also lower-powered machines like the Dodge Colt. Even semi-exotics like the BMW 2002 joined the party. Pinto's good showing in IMSA came courtesy of *Car and Driver* magazine, including the journal's resident hotshoe racing driver Patrick Bedard.

The Bob Glidden Pinto was painted in Stars & Stripes livery during the 1975 and 1976 racing seasons. The color scheme came courtesy of Glidden's partner, Bob Allen. While painted red, this Pinto set a 1974 P/S national record of 8.83 seconds at 154.90mph. (Courtesy www.mecum.com)

The Ford Pinto also participated in Trans Am racing, following in the tire tracks of its Boss Mustang big brother. The category was the SCCA's 2-5 Challenge. (Courtesy Rudy Flores Galpin Auto Sports galpinautosports.com)

Above: Bert Boeckman's major SoCal Ford dealership, Galpin Ford, took up the SCCA's 2-5 Challenge with alacrity. Galpin sold Pintos, so why not race 'em?! (Courtesy Rudy Flores Galpin Auto Sports galpinautosports.com)

Left: In a long racing career, the 2-5 Challenge Pinto continued until 2010. It was then rediscovered by the Galpin Group, becoming part of the Galpin Auto Sports collection. The car has never been restored, and still features its original paint and decals. (Courtesy Rudy Flores Galpin Auto Sports galpinautosports.com)

Ford Mustang II & Pinto

Thanks to *Car and Driver* magazine, and racing scribe Patrick Bedard, the Ford Pinto had a successful foray in the 1974 IMSA B F Goodrich Radial Challenge. The journal had winningly competed with a Mazda RX2 in 1973. (Courtesy Marc Noordeloos www.foxmotorsports.com)

C/D and Bedard were winning IMSA participants during the 1973 racing season, using a Mazda RX-2. Unfortunately, it won too well. Their success invited rival protests and close IMSA scrutiny. The upshot was a weight penalty, and eventual ban on rotary engine porting. The latter rendered the RX-2 uncompetitive. Building on the great experience gained racing the RX-2 in 1973, *C/D* plus Bedard turned to the Ford Pinto for 1974; but why? There were two main reasons. Firstly, the journal wished to show an intelligent, commonsense approach to racing would yield dividends. Without resorting to a big budget, and super famous racing driver. Secondly, Ford's Pinto was quite a sound machine, with good qualities that made it well-suited to the business at hand.

C/D observed frontal area, weight, displacement, handling, wheel width and horsepower versus other potential vehicle choices. The journal concluded a 2.3-liter

Car and Driver was advised by Doug Fraser Racing Engines that the 2.3-liter Lima had greater potential than its sedan's stock 2-liter mill. The modification put Pinto into the faster class of IMSA racers, and brought a 200lb rulebook weight penalty. (Courtesy Marc Noordeloos www.foxmotorsports.com)

Pinto sedan could be a contender. Engine work was delegated to Doug Fraser Racing Engines of Marblehead Massachusetts. This firm advised that the 2.3-liter Lima motor offered superior ports, with greater tuning potential than the normal 2-liter Pinto I4. The smaller motor came with the used car *C/D* had purchased for its endeavor. The car in question was a 1972 Pinto with 30,000 miles on the odometer. It was a two year old two-door sedan in neat condition,

and came with the familiar German four-speed Hummer gearbox.

In going with the 2.3 Lima motor, and choosing to run with the more powerful cars in the Radial Challenge, *C/D* accepted the rulebook's added 200lb weight penalty. As per the '73 racing season RX-2, *C/D* co-driver and race car builder for the Pinto exercise was Ron Nash. Most of the car's race preparation work was carried out in the *Car and Driver* workshop. Valuable advice came from Ford chassis engineer Bob Negstad. Negstad was seminal in Pinto and Mustang II's chassis design. He had set up the former for circle track racing previously. Negstad suggested the '74 Pinto's steering gear. He also advised applying the larger 1974 front disks to the '72 machine, another good retrofit.

The *C/D* Pinto utilized a Vette radiator, and Hurst shifter, along with a 4.10 or 4.30 rear axle, depending on the circuit at hand. Koni shocks were used at the front, Bilsteins on the rear. An optimized rollcage, with carefully selected attachment points improved the unibody's rigidity. Trials to set the car up

Car and Driver **purchased a two-year-old '72 Pinto sedan with 30,000 miles, for the IMSA series. Expertise for the project came from Ford chassis guru Bob Negstad, and racing ace Mark Donohue. The latter designed the Pinto's racing seat. So, *C/D* Pinto really had that unfair advantage! (Courtesy Marc Noordeloos www.foxmotorsports.com)**

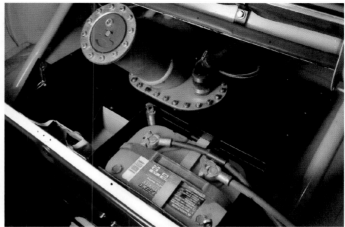

involved half a day on the skidpad, and the same amount of time running around the Lime Rock race circuit. The *C/D* Pinto made its racing debut at Talladega, and completed its first race.

The *Car and Driver* Pinto did four races during the '74 racing season. It recorded two pole positions, and Bedard achieved one victory. This win was the Pinto's second race, held at Charlotte Motor Speedway. It was Pinto's first B F Goodrich Radial Challenge win in two years of competition. In Bedard's opinion, Pinto was tops concerning cornering on a tight dry track. The wide front and rear tracks, both 55in, were an asset. In Patrick Bedard's words: "It's a great car to drive, this Pinto." (March 1975 *Car and Driver*)

Once *Car and Driver* achieved its 1974 racing objective, the car was sold to privateer Bob Leier. Leier used the Pinto in some '75 racing season IMSA and Canadian races. The little sedan then sat for 30 years in Virginia, after a final race outing at Daytona. In 2005, *Car and Driver*'s editor Don Sherman oversaw a nine month restoration of the *C/D* Pinto. The Ford then joined the Fox Motorsports Collection in September 2007.

The *C/D* Pinto originally raced on steel rims, but as part of the restoration Sherman added BWA alloys. A racing car of considerable historical note, the *C/D* Pinto's racing seat was designed by the great racer and engineer Mark Donohue. *Car and Driver* wasn't the only one trusting Pinto. Jerry Walsh was already competing in the Baby Grand IMSA class.

In more recent times, the SCCA's Washington DC regional Pinto series is further proof the diminutive Ford is a safe, budget-minded entry to the world of motorsport. Circle track racing can provide an economical entry point to

Above: The *C/D* Pinto did four races in the 1974 racing season. The subcompact had a successful tally of two pole positions, and a win at Charlotte Motor Speedway. The exercise proved that sensible budget racing could work. It also showed that Pinto's wide track made it a demon handler. (Courtesy Marc Noordeloos www.foxmotorsports.com)

Below: In 2005, former *Car and Driver* editor Don Sherman oversaw restoration of the *C/D* Pinto. The car was given BWA aluminum rims, and subsequently became part of the Fox Motorsports Collection for several years. (Courtesy Marc Noordeloos www.foxmotorsports.com)

motorsport too. The Pinto's popularity in the Pony Stock junior racing division is an example. As mentioned by Steve Smith in the February 2009 issue of *Circle Track*, policeman Lou Gamache was a competitive racer on a budget. A resident of San Bernardino, Californian Gamache raced his Pinto at Orange Show Speedway.

NASCAR – The 'Rapid Roman' Pinto

Racer Richie Evans started working and racing in Rome, New York. That location and his success inspired his nickname, the Rapid Roman. As a backstory regarding his orange painted No 61 racers, Evans once worked for the county. Legend has it, some county property once went missing. Concerning such orange paint, the rest is history!

A major success in his racing domain, Richie Evans won nine NASCAR National Modified Championships. He garnered over 400 victories in the process. One of Evans' famous racecraft was an orange colored No 61 tubeframe racer, with a small-block Chevy 427 V8.

This successful racing car was based, albeit loosely, on a Ford Pinto. Evans' Pinto-based machine was painted Ford Grabber Orange. He was always careful concerning primer usage, because it easily bled through with an orange exterior. To this end, he used red oxide primer. Such primer merely tinted the orange exterior a little darker. That orange shade was complemented by equally famous black numerals with white shading. When a Roman wants to be rapid, he moves from Torino to Pinto!

The Pinto arrived during Ford's 'Total Performance Era.' Win on Sunday, sell on Monday. However, things were changing. (Courtesy Ford Motor Co)

When Ford spent $250,000 on this experimental car, they weren't about to cut corners on the oil filter. So they used an Autolite filter.

Like you buy. Under $4.

From the ground to the roll bar, this car is only three feet tall. It was built by Ford to test new design concepts. At a cost of $250,000. The movable control panel cost $10,000. (It adjusts to the driver.) The hand-formed aluminum body cost $50,000.

And the oil filter? Less than $4. It's an Autolite oil filter. The same kind *you* buy. What's a $4 Autolite oil filter doing in a $250,000 car? Simple. There *is* no better filter at *any* price.

The Autolite filter is a two-stage filter. A depth filter that removes up to ten times as much dirt and sludge as ordinary filters. It can actually *double the life* of your oil. What's more, it has an up-front bypass valve to prevent trapped dirt from washing back into your engine.

So put this kind of filter in your kind of car. Whatever kind you drive. Autolite ... the only name you need to know for filters, spark plugs, batteries, shock absorbers and complete ignition systems.

Autolite *Ford*

Appendix

The Sudden Death Mustang II

In spite of the Big Brother actions of the federal government, enthusiasts across the land were improving their cars, just as they always had. Shoehorning a larger emissions-legal motor into a smaller ride was a logical route. To overcome the pollution controlled times, some enterprising souls snaked 302s into their little cars, and big blocks into Mustang II – Gapp & Roush were involved with the latter scenario. Private requests were done by racing outfits between meets, as part of their commercial business.

As recounted by the October 1975 issue of *Super Stock and Drag Illustrated*, with reference to the popular '75 summer movie *Jaws*, the article was titled, 'Jaws – Putting some real teeth in a Mustang II.' Wayne Gapp explained: "Well, we take on occasional projects for people, just to keep my crew busy when I don't need them for the race cars."[10] In the workshop was a new '75 Mustang II fastback, still in possession of its window sticker. However, it wore 12in rear slicks and was bereft of its front sheet metal! It was a car for property developer Joe Ruggirello, who wanted a machine faster than his old street racer Torino. For 12 grand this could be done.

The motor was a 460 Super Cobra Jet that had received a 0.030in overbore. Gapp allowed as to how they put high comp pistons and strong cam into the motor, plus ported and polished the 429 SCJ heads. The motor backed onto a

The Sudden Death Mustang II got its moniker from an article written by *Hot Rod*'s Gray Baskerville. It was a custom big block street racer, created by Gapp & Roush for property tycoon Joe Ruggirello. (Courtesy Tom Tate)

A stock 1975 Mustang II/ Pinto steering wheel, but Sudden Death's engine was something else. The car's motor went through an evolution of bored-out 429 SCJ (460ci), through 505 cubes, and then enjoyed twin turbos! It eventually returned to its 505ci V8 form. (Courtesy Tom Tate)

1972 C6 automatic with Winters 4000 stall torque converter. A Ford 9-inch with 4.30 rear gears could handle the power. With help from a narrowed housing that contained a Detroit Locker lsd. To accommodate the giant V8, Gapp & Roush notched the cowl. In moving the big-block back 10in, a custom firewall was created, and torque boxes were used to beef up chassis strength. Pro Stock (P/S) type engine mounts were used on this P/S style street car. The fastback sat on a round tube frame, and the rear had been tubbed to fit monster-sized rubber. This necessitated inboard movement of the live axle's leafs. Those rear covers were Firestone Drag 500s of 29.5 x 15in dimensions on machine finish rims. The fronts saw four-bolt 13 x 6in ET Slots and Goodyear D70-13 Polyglas tires. Such front footwear has been discontinued.

Then there were little details like fiberglass front and rear bumpers. Both had a gel coat finish, and the whole car was painted in various shades of Ford Metallic Silver. The engine also affected cosmetics. Not the JR headers with 1⅞in primary diameter tubes, but the Shelby dual plane intake and 850 CFM double pumper Holley. As Wayne Gapp

Famous Gapp & Roush alumni. Sudden Death (background) shares workshop space with the Gapp & Roush Tijuana Taxi. The famous Tijuana Taxi was a winning SOHC 427 V8-powered Maverick. (Courtesy Tom Tate & Norman Blake)

Below: The cost to Joe Ruggirello was around 12 grand. The peace of mind from being the ultimate street door slammer was priceless! A Shelby dual plane intake and Holley 850 CFM double pumper, turned dreams into reality. During restoration, the carb was upgraded to 930 CFM. (Courtesy Tom Tate)

told *Super Stock and Drag Illustrated*: "I guess we'll have to put a little scoop on it. That's the only thing wrong with it – we can't get the damn thing shut." Unusually for the era, the hoodscoop was functional – everything on the car was functional. The stock interior, with normal '75 Mustang II/Pinto tiller, didn't talk either. Place your foot on the loud pedal, and 10 seconds at 140mph said plenty!

In the April 1977 issue of *Hot Rod* magazine, Gray Baskerville named Joe Ruggirello's '75 Mustang II, licence plate RNL589, 'Sudden Death.' It was sudden death to anyone dumb enough to take this street racer on, and it didn't stop there. The car was a work in progress. A year or so later, Sudden Death returned to Gapp & Roush for a 4.15in stroke, offset ground crank, Carillo rods and 505 cubes. By now there was 13 grand invested in the project. A 600ci all-alloy Ford Can Am short-block was on standby, but no. Come 1980/81, the hot Mustang II was back to G&R for twin turbos!

By 1981, Sudden Death was still owned by Mr. Ruggirello, who had put his mother's name Josephine on the original Ford Motor Credit title. The fastback then went through several hands, and was eventually spotted in white with blue stripes livery by Tom Tate. The car happened to be at the 1995 Fun Ford Weekend at Gainesville Raceway. Tate then spent the next 15 years searching, and finally found Sudden Death for sale in 2010. It had been in semi storage for 10 years in New Jersey. It still had the twin turbos, but needed restoration. This act Mr Tate did accomplish, saving this very historically significant car for all enthusiasts. The decision was taken by Tom Tate, to return Sudden Death to 1977 505ci non-turbo form. Close to the car Gray Baskerville wrote about.

Above: A notched cowl and custom firewall allowed Gapp & Roush to move the big block V8 back 10in. Sudden Death sat on a round tube frame. The rear was tubbed, and leaf springs were moved inboard to make room for monster rubber. A Ford nine inch with narrowed housing, and Detroit Locker lsd, handled the power. (Courtesy Tom Tate)

Below: As observed by Sudden Death's restorer, Tom Tate, this iconic machine has historical custodians rather than owners. Sudden Death is an acknowledged seminal street racer, whose legend continues to grow. (Courtesy Tom Tate)

Pavement Pounder Pinto – V8 street & cruise night special

Above: Dick Kashdin's 1972 blown Pavement Pounder Pinto was inspired by a drag racing caricature, and started as a real life drag racer in the 1970s. Today, it's strictly for street use, no racing, but does have a 600 horse blown Windsor 305. (Courtesy Dick Kashdin)

Below: A Dyer 6-71 supercharger provides the Windsor V8's forced induction. Belt clearance is minimal, and an Opel four cylinder motor water pump, plus other mods, allows everything to just fit underhood! (Courtesy Dick Kashdin)

From the moment the Ford Pinto came out, racers and enthusiasts started snaking Windsor and Cleveland V8s into the little subcompact's engine compartment. Whether it was a professional Pro Stocker, pink slip seeking street racer, or car customizer, the Pinto was often teamed up with a FoMoCo V8. This was the case with Dick Kashdin's 1972 blown Pinto, which started as a drag racer in 1977. It was raced until 1992, when regulations required major rollcage changes. The decision was made to avoid the regs, and just use the Pinto for local drag strip work and street machine action.

The Pinto subsequently sat dormant, until a further decision was made in 2010 to retire the car from all racing, and convert it into a street machine and cruise night car. To go from racer to a reliable street car compliant with federal safety regulations involves a tremendous amount of work. This certainly proved the case with Kashdin's car. Inspiration came from a Pinto street machine caricature, and originally three very real Pinto donor cars, to make the original drag racer. Back in the '70s, said Pintos were sourced from junkyards and collision shops.

The motor is a completely cast iron 1977 Ford 302, bored out 0.030in to almost 305ci. As a forced induction 302, it has 8.5:1 TRW flat-forged pistons, and a Scat-forged crankshaft. The worked

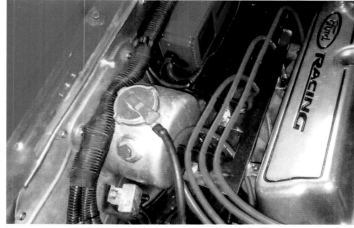

heads have had an angled valve job, plus hardened valve seats. Port flow stainless steel valves are sized 2.2in on the intake side, and 1.7in on the exhaust side. Valvegear incorporates Harland Sharp 1.6:1 roller rockers, ⅜in screw-in studs, guide plates and stud girdles. To keep those 16 pushrods pleased, a Crane hydraulic roller camshaft is employed. It has 226 degrees of intake duration at 0.050in of lift, 236 degrees of exhaust duration at 0.050in of lift. There is 0.502in of intake valve lift and 0.520in exhaust valve lift with 110 degree lobe center and the valves set at zero lash. Carburetion is by 600 CFM Edelbrock dual quads. These supply the Dyer 6-71 blower, which sits on a custom aluminum single plane high rise intake manifold.

With the blower 8% under-driven and 10psi boost, the result is over 600 horses.

Fitting the abovementioned V8 in a manner resembling a factory fit was a challenge. Firstly, the front clip was removed and disassembled. The front frame was beefed up, and Ford 302 V8 engine mounts were placed so the firewall and surrounding engine compartment parts would have minimal disruption. Tight underhood space saw a custom adaptor from Californian company Snow White; this permitted an Opel 1.9-liter engine water pump to be used with the 302 V8. Matching the Opel water pump's passenger side inlet needed a Chevy radiator, which has the bottom radiator outlet on the lower passenger side. This led to modifying

To make Pavement Pounder Pinto safe and reliable in its conversion from race car to street car, the entire electrical system was inspected and modified. A MSD Blaster 2 coil has joined a Ford distributor, and unlike a stock '72 Pinto sedan, Pavement Pounder Pinto now has a horn relay. (Courtesy Dick Kashdin)

The Pavement Pounder Pinto retains the stock voltage regulator location. The braking system master cylinder, and vacuum booster, are also visible. (Courtesy Dick Kashdin)

Ford Mustang II & Pinto

Top: Inside Pavement Pounder Pinto, the 600 plus horse blown 302 Windsor is controlled by a C4 automatic topped by a B&M shifter. The C4 has Kevlar clutches, and a neutral safety switch. (Courtesy Dick Kashdin)

Bottom: The cowl gages inform the driver of fuel pressure, transmission fluid temp, and blower boost psi. Angled dashboard gages provide more info. A custom console control panel has switches to activate various ancillaries. (Courtesy Dick Kashdin)

the Ford radiator support brackets, and sourcing radiator hoses to fit. A pusher electric fan saves space, and the battery was relocated rearwards.

Changes to carburetion over the years, plus fuel line positions, meant hood mechanism modifications were needed. To get the hood to fit involved many hours of hand grinding and filing work. The final result was the product of trial and error. Tabs for the hood's flush head fasteners were welded on. Repositioning mod work also applied to the ignition system. This set-up now encompasses a MSD 6AL box with 6000rpm chip, MSD Blaster 2 coil, working with a largely stock Ford

distributor with 8mm plug wires and Champion RV8C sparkplugs. The voltage regulator was kept on the driver's side inner fender, for appearance.

Possibly thanks to bean counter economies, the 1972 Pinto didn't have a horn relay. The ground for the standard horn was through the attachment screw, into the passenger side inner fender. The horn drew power from under the dash. There was a wire to one side of the horn button on the steering column. A fused wire went to the horn button's other side, it was then through the firewall to the horn's positive side. As part of this Pinto's street car conversion, power goes to a horn relay. The horn button on the

steering column is now the ground to activate the horn relay and 12-volt power source.

The transmission is a C4 automatic with Kevlar clutches, worked via a B&M shifter. Due to further economies, the '72 Pinto four-speed lacked a neutral safety switch. Now one was needed for the B&M shifter. Exhaust work is taken care of by Blackjack headers, with four equal length primary pipes, going into 3in primary collectors, then 3in exhaust tubes, going into a 3in 'H-style' crossover, then 3in pipes to Flowmaster 40 Series mufflers, which end in front of the rear rubber. A Currie Custom differential involved a narrowed big bearing Ford 9in with 31 spline Currie axles. In racing days, the car used a 4.11:1 Currie gearset. This was changed to a Currie 3.70:1 Positraction for street use. The change necessitated longer Currie custom axles to reach the Positraction clutches.

To monitor safe performance of engine and transmission, three left-to-right cowl gages covering fuel pressure/transmission temp/boost psi are visible to the driver. In its past incarnation as a drag car, modifications and various splices had been done to the electrical system. As a dedicated racer, this suited its purpose, and things like the horn could be disconnected. To be street safe, the entire electrical system had to be examined. This necessitated dropping the steering column and removing the center dash pad. The wiring for the angled gages (from left to right: fuel, coolant temp, oil pressure, battery charge) was inspected too. The heater/blower control dash area was plated over, and a custom console control panel with switches/fuses was added. This covered fuel pump, pusher fan and water pump activation, with extra functions addable if necessary.

When the original drag car was created in 1977, the back half was provided by the third donor car – a Pinto sedan. Pinto sedans were considered better than their hatchback counterparts,

Pavement Pounder Pinto's specs run to four wheel disk brakes and coil over suspension. The car has been tubbed, and has rear 18.8in wide Hoosier Pro Street tires. (Courtesy Dick Kashdin)

due to superior body rigidity. Also in vogue back in 1977 was the chosen ladder bar rear suspension. A 1in by 3in channel steel frame tied the bottom of the front and center sections to the rear half.

The eight point roll cage also helped join center and rear half sections. Stock Pinto rack and pinion steering, plus inner fenders, were retained. Front suspension went to coil overs. Also part of the two year conversion from drag racer to street machine was the use of five lug rotor disk brakes and coilovers at all four corners. Rear wheel tubs are 19.5in deep, housing Hoosier Pro Street 31in high and 18.8in wide tires. The tires are mounted on 15in aluminum Weld Wheels with spinners.

The battery, battery shut off switch, fuel lines and 12-gallon foam-filled JAZ fuel cell, fuel filter and fuel pump all live in the trunk. The filter and pump are under the trunk, toward the passenger side. The fuel cell has a fuel sensor for the fuel gage – another sign of street use. Refinements have seen a power radio antenna frenched into the passenger side rear fender. The original drag aluminum rear wing is now covered in red carbon fiber look wrap. The parachute has been removed, but the old school spring type wheelie bars remain. A legacy from the days when this Pinto used to do sub ten second passes at nearly 150mph!

Pavement Pounder Pinto utilizes a 12 gallon foam-filled JAZ fuel cell. The car was originally constructed from three Pintos in the '70s. A sedan was chosen due to its superior structural rigidity. Today, the rear spoiler is covered with a red carbon-fiber-look wrap. (Courtesy Dick Kashdin)

Famous & infamous Pintos

In the TV show *Charlie's Angels*, character Sabrina Duncan drove the orange Pinto Runabout, and passed it on to replacement angel Tiffany Welles (actress Shelley Hack). In the episode 'One Love … Two Angels,' Welles rented another Pinto. This beige car got crushed on a construction site, when an attempt was made on her life! The orange Pinto was safely parked outside the Charles Townsend Detective Agency at the time. The Runabout was then driven by its final custodian Julie Rogers (actress Tanya Roberts), in the fifth and final 1980-81 season of the show. The whereabouts of this orange Pinto is unknown.

A Pinto featured prominently in the 1996-97 first season episode 'Wrecking Crew' of the TV show *Nash Bridges*. Here, Inspectors Bridges and Dominguez were doing moonlighting investigative work, trying to locate a missing 1973 Pinto hatchback. The car was the goodluck charm of fictitious baseball star Rondell, played by Barry Bonds. By the show's end, Inspector Nash Bridges used the Pinto to ram through a building, save Joe Dominguez and foil the bad guys.

In the 1980 movie *The Blues Brothers*, a Pinto was driven by the bad guys, a couple of Neo Nazis who were chasing Jake and Elwood. The bad guys in the Pinto wagon met a grizzly end, when it fell from a great height. In the 1974 cop show *Police Woman* episode 'The Stalking of Joey Marr,' Sgt Leanne 'Pepper' Anderson (Angie Dickinson) rented a lime green Pinto wagon, while protecting mobster Marr (Monte Markham) who was going to testify in court. The Pinto wagon overheated when chased by mob killers.

There was additional FoMoCo product placement, in the first season of *Police Woman*. In the episode 'Fish,' a smurf blue Mustang II fastback was T-boned by Detective Styles' police car. In the episode 'Ice,' Pepper and her boss Lieutenant Crowley take a trip down to Mexico undercover, and rent a green 1967 Mustang hardtop. In the same episode, actor Michael Parks looks out the window to see a new '74 green Mustang II Ghia hardtop being driven away. The shades of green were similar, and FoMoCo seemed to want to build a connection between Mustangs old and new.

The AVE Mizar was a high flying Pinto, which turned out to be a low flyer. It was the creation of Advanced Vehicle Engineers (AVE), a company that was based in Van Nuys, Los Angeles. The company was started by Henry Smolinski. A partner in the firm was Bert Boeckmann, owner of big dealer Galpin Ford. Mizar prototypes involved joining a Cessna Skymaster airframe to a Pinto. AVE planned to have its own custom built airframe done, but for the moment (1971-73), Cessna hardware was handy. One prototype was on display at Galpin Ford. It was a static display.

The other proto with 210 horse Teledyne Continental Motors (TCM) engine, was shown to the press on May 8 1973. The total package weighed slightly more than a Skymaster. The intention was to use the TCM engine, plus the Pinto's car motor to assist with take off. The car's brakes would bring it to a halt on landing. The airframe would then be unbolted, allowing the Pinto to be driven off. At 1973 prices the car/plane would be 25 grand, when a Mercedes 280 compact was $9000. On test flights there was trouble with the right wing strut base mounting attachment.

On the August 26 1973 test flight, from Camarillo Airport, the attachment failure caused the test pilot Charles 'Red' Janisse to set the Mizar down. The same problem occurred on September 11 1973, at the same airport. This time, company founder Henry Smolinski unwisely tried to turn, according to Janisse, and the wing folded. The fatal

In the TV show *Charlie's Angels*, character Sabrina Duncan drove a Pinto Runabout hatch, that looked very similar to this 24 Hours of LeMons racer. (Courtesy Murilee Martin autoweek.com)

The Pinto's familiar 2.3-liter Lima I4 made a '74 MY debut. However, this Runabout's motor was lifted from an '80s Thunderbird Turbo. SVO took the inline four on to 200bhp! (Courtesy Murilee Martin autoweek.com)

This Pinto Turbo belongs to Bill Rainey of the Sabrina Duncan's Revenge Race Team. 1978 was the final year for Pinto's Maverick matching styling. (Courtesy Murilee Martin autoweek.com)

Left: Genuine era plaid Pinto trim went well with the Tangerine Orange and Polar White exterior. Not very ingognito for a Townsend Detective Agency vehicle! (Courtesy Murilee Martin autoweek.com)

Below: The full glass hatch gave the Runabout a more modern appearance. The Townsend Detective Agency Pinto proved very reliable. It served no fewer than three *Angels* between 1976 and 1981. (Courtesy Murilee Martin autoweek.com)

crash claimed the life of Smolinski and AVE Vice President Harold Blake.

The crash investigation by the National Transportation Safety Board (NTSB) found poor design, loose parts and bad welding. The crash ended the venture, along with the Mizar's intended use in the 1974 Bond film *The Man With*

The Golden Gun. It had been planned for assassin Scaramanga and henchman Nick Nack to escape Bond in a Mizar. Instead they rigged up Scaramanga's AMC Matador Coupe to look like it could fly. A radio-controlled scale model was then utilized for flight shots.

Pinto safety – unfairly accused

Independent sources of review, using publicly available car accident data, have shown the Ford Pinto to have the same level of crash safety as its small car contemporaries. In a 1991 Rutgers Law Review study, UCLA law professor Gary T Schwartz, provided the fact that during 1975-76, the Pinto represented 1.9% of the North American car population. The Pinto was also involved in 1.9% of crash fatalities, involving fire. This showed the Pinto to be quite normal, concerning fire-related deaths in the small car class, during a time when said car was at its peak popularity on North American roads.

It is a further fact that fire-related rear end car crashes make up a very small percentage of car deaths. Observing the 1970 to mid 1977 period, the NHTSA (National Highway Traffic Safety Administration) discerned 27 fatalities concerning fire-related crashes, involving the Ford Pinto. However, given over 3 million Pintos were sold, the number of fire-related deaths were consistent with the car industry average. The 27 fatalities discerned by the NHTSA government body, was nowhere near the 500-900 deaths claimed by journalist Mark Dowie in his August 1977 *Mother Jones* article 'Pinto Madness.'

The number of fire-related crash fatalities concerning Pinto was still 27 at the time of the Professor Schwartz article. The study also showed that for accidents of all types, the Ford Pinto was slightly better than the small car average of its era. It was equal to domestic rivals Vega and Gremlin, as well as the Datsun

510. Ford Pinto clearly outperformed the smaller Datsun 1200/210 (120Y), Corolla and the VW Beetle. The more recent investigative study by Professor of Engineering Mark Rossow, 'Ethics: An Alternative Account of the Ford Pinto Case' (2015), also confirms the assertion that Pinto was as safe as small car rivals, and even safer in some aspects.

How did a small car that was legally safe for sale, and proven equal to the level of passive safety offered by rivals, come to be singled out as a hazardous vehicle? Unfortunately, a combination of adversarial litigation, active safety lobby group, out of control media and pressured government authority, all conspired to create a witch hunt that unfairly tarnished the Pinto's safety image. In a way, Pinto's popularity and the fact it was made by the world's second biggest car company, made the Pinto and Ford a litigation target. It was all a feeding frenzy for mainstream media sharks.

Ford Pinto was a very big-selling automobile. In 1974 BMW sold 15,000 cars in North America, Pontiac sold nearly 74,000 Firebirds. However, Ford sold 544,209 Pintos in 1974. Even the VW Beetle, the single best-selling car design of all time, couldn't match Pinto's peak American sales. Beetle's best year was 1968. That year, the Vee Dub managed 390,379 units Stateside. It's a perspective many overlooked. Chances are, when you sell that many cars, a few people, relatively speaking, are going to have some very bad accidents. The other fact to consider is that it is an agreed tenet of auto safety that in a crash between a smaller, lighter car and a heavier, larger vehicle, all other factors being constant (ceteris paribus), occupants of the smaller car have a greater chance of serious injury than those of the larger vehicle. It is also agreed in auto safety that, all other factors held constant, a larger, heavier car provides better passive crash safety than a smaller, lighter vehicle.

All of the above was continued in the tragic case of Grimshaw v Ford Motor Co. Here a 1972 Pinto driven by Mrs Lilly Gray stalled on a Californian freeway, and was rear-ended by a '62 Ford Galaxie. In common with other federal pollution-controlled cars of the era, Mrs Gray's Pinto had suffered continual stalling problems, which her dealer was unable to cure. Shortly before the accident she had filled up with gas, so the tank was pretty full.

The Galaxie driver had no opportunity to swerve or slow down, and struck the Pinto while traveling at between 30 and 50mph. The severe impact force pushed the Pinto's gas tank forward, it ruptured when striking the rear differential's bolts, and gasoline entered the passenger compartment when the rear wheel well sections separated from the floor pan. Mrs Gray subsequently died from her injuries, and child passenger Richard Grimshaw suffered severe burns. The jury awarded $127.8 million in total damages, and so commenced the witch hunt.

Objectively, a similar result would have occurred if the Galaxie struck any small car of the era. That is, a scenario where a 2000lb car measuring 160in in length is struck by a 4000lb fullsize car over 210in long. It also seems likely that if the car involved was a X1/9, and the automaker was Fiat, the same course of litigation and media hoopla wouldn't have happened. However, half a million X1/9s weren't sold in 1972 America, and Fiat was not Ford. Critics were quick to brand the Pinto unsafe, when no one really knew what safe was; certainly not the NHTSA.

During the Ford Pinto's development and initial release, and for a good time thereafter, the government body hadn't decided yet what constituted a reasonable rear end crash test, and therefore what was a safe car. During Pinto development, the NHTSA proposed a moving barrier 20mph rear impact test, like the 5mph bumper basher test only more so. A vehicle with a large board would strike a stationary test subject at 20mph. Ford and other automakers were okay with this, and designed the Pinto accordingly.

Unfortunately for Ford and other automakers, the NHTSA subsequently decided the test should be made stricter. Just prior to the Pinto's September 1970 release, the NHTSA decided the proposed standard should be a fixed barrier 20mph rear end crash. Here, the car is towed backwards into the barrier, like the NHTSA's familiar frontal crash except in reverse. All the automakers protested this stricter proposal. Shortly thereafter the NHTSA made the proposal stricter still: it was now up to a 30mph fixed barrier rear ender. The government just plain couldn't make up its mind!

The NHTSA said the 30mph fixed barrier standard may have been introduced for '77 model year. In the meantime, Ford set its sights on the 20mph moving barrier standard for '73 MY, because this proposal seemed the most likely to become actual law. FoMoCo reached this decision in early 1971. Eventually, the NHTSA agreed the fixed barrier test was too unrealistic and overly strict, and went for the moving barrier option, for any immediate proposed legal standard. It doesn't make sense for one company to design its product beyond an actual legal standard, in a competitive market place. Rivals, like Japanese imports that didn't, would be placed at an advantage in terms of avoiding design costs. They would also possess a lighter, more fuel-efficient automobile, that may price out lower. American Motors made its Pacer overly heavy, and designed its unibody to cope with a proposed federal rollover crash standard that never came. As a result, the model was placed at a competitive disadvantage, versus more economical, lighter imports. Poor Pacer was criticized for its size and weight.

Ford felt it was prudent to seek clarification on proposed laws, and design the Pinto in terms of likely federal standards. Unfortunately, *Mother Jones*' Mark Dowie spent some time at the DOT (Dept of Transportation), and discovered a document that he felt showed Ford had blood on its hands. He certainly presented his finding in this manner, and many took his word as the gospel truth. Dowie alleged Ford did cost-benefit analysis on a Pinto redesign concerning rear end collision fires, and decided it was cheaper to do court cases than redesign the car and make it 'safe,' whatever exactly that was.

The so-called 'Pinto Death Memo' he found and his 'Pinto Madness' article became a veritable lightning rod for every disaffected individual and group that ever had a beef with corporate America. The unfortunate Pinto became their whipping boy of choice. The Pulitzer committee awarded Dowie for his sterling effort in finding the only unsafe car on America's roads. They no doubt petitioned the Vatican for his immediate canonization. How could he be wrong? Aren't corporations judged evil until proven innocent?

Well, it turned out that the Pinto Death Memo, wasn't actually a death memo. When the NHTSA was trying to decide a rear end crash safety standard, the body invited written responses from automakers, seeking their opinion concerning proposed laws. Ford's Environmental And Safety Engineering Division submitted a document in 1973. It concerned improved designs for rollover testing. The document concerned all vehicles and all automakers selling their products in North America. It did not specifically concern Ford, or

the Pinto, it was a general briefing that discussed raising standards in auto safety. The possible real world improvements in safety from doing so, as well as the increased financial burdens placed on companies and consumers, were also considered.

Someone has to pay for redesign work, and down the line car prices would be higher. It was wise to work out if real safety gains would result from legislative change, prior to such laws being passed. In creating its document Ford used industry and NHTSA used and accepted cost-benefit analysis. Indeed, the $200,000 per life figure was done by the NHTSA in 1972. In addition, while these proposed legal changes were up for discussion, Ford had tried design improvements on its Maverick and Pinto. They were of similar nature, to the changes effected upon Pinto during its 1978 recall. Ford found that concerning a 30mph fixed barrier, rear end crash test, such modifications would be of limited value.

Using the technology of the day, it was very difficult and perhaps impossible to create a small car that could withstand a rear end hit from a vehicle weighing over 4000lb, traveling at 30mph or greater. Ford had a good track record in passive safety. The company had offered lap belt restraints and other measures very early on, but most buyers weren't interested. Hence the Ford statement that safety didn't sell. Ford was at the forefront in adopting crumple zones in the design of new cars. Up there with Volvo and BMW, even though in the mid to late '60s some experts thought a rigid separate chassis was better.

For 1972 model year Ford designed the new separate chassis Gran Torino, with a frame that gave. Computer design made this frame part crumple and absorb crash energy, to protect vehicle occupants. Sadly, the federal 5mph bumper standard of 1973 forced Ford to straighten the front frame's 'S' shaped members, so that stuff like a/c condensers and radiators would be protected. The federal government was listening to insurance company lobbyists, and thought it was better to protect cars, not people.

The Pinto had been criticized for its gas tank placement between rear axle and bumper. However, as noted by Autoweek's Mike Bumbeck and many others, this gas tank placement was normal for small cars of the time. Pinto critics have mentioned the saddlebag type gas tank as being preferable. Here the tank is placed over and shaped around the rear axle, to provide more crush space. However, opinion was divided on its virtue. The engineer overseeing Pinto's design was Harold MacDonald. MacDonald felt a saddlebag tank, apart from placing gas closer to occupants, could also get punctured by trunk

contents and was potentially equally dangerous in a hatchback. Bearing out his reasoning, two new cars came out in North America for '77 MY with the saddlebag gas tank, the BMW 320i and Mercedes W123, both were sedans. Interestingly, MacDonald had lost his father to a fire-related auto accident. His father's Ford Model A had struck a tree.

There were a number of cars on sale with potential hazards during the Pinto's era. Gas tanks forming the floors of trunks (VW Beetle), exposed gas filler tubing in the trunk compartment (Chrysler A body), rear deck mounted gas filler (Pontiac Firebird 1967-81 & BMW 530i 1975-76). However, it seemed the central safety lobby group, Ralph Nader's Center for Auto Safety, only had eyes for the Ford Pinto. Then on August

Well, at least someone had a sense of humor! The Ford Pinto's small car safety reputation was unfairly maligned by safety zealots and anti Big Three sentiment. (Courtesy Joe Kruskamp)

10 1977, there occurred an unholy alliance between a safety zealot and a doomsday scaremonger, in that political utopia known as Washington D.C. Ralph Nader and Mark Dowie gave a solemn press conference, warning the public of "alleged Pinto dangers." If only this dynamic duo were equally concerned about other potential auto hazards.

Nader's 1960s book *Unsafe At Any Speed* had finished off the Chevy Corvair's image. Like Pinto, the Corvair was an economy car attempt to take on VW's Bug. Like Beetle, the Corvair had a rear-mounted engine, and independent suspension that would oversteer on the limit, not the usual understeer folks were raised on. Some cases of incorrectly inflated tire pressures, and domestic car owners not used to such rear-engined fare, led to accidents that Nader focused on. The Corvair was unfairly described as unsafe at any speed. Thankfully, this didn't phase Don Yenko, who made his Corvair-based Stinger sportster, which predated those famous Camaros. The swing-axled Beetle also had a reputation for flipping over. However, Volkswagen made the Beetle, not mighty Chevrolet. Nader wasn't overly concerned with imported Bugs in 1977.

Ralph Nader and his Center for Auto Safety wrecking crew, had trashed Herbie earlier in the decade. In September 1971 they had released the report 'The Volkswagen: An Assessment of Distinctive Hazards.' In this report Nader & Co attacked the Beetle and VW Microbus/Van, raising concerns with crash safety, handling and a propensity to go 'Up In Flames' – sound familiar? In April 1972 *Road & Track* looked closely at this report, interviewed Nader and his posse, and concluded the study was factually selective, and very unfair concerning VW safety.

Nader and Dowie also seemed ignorant of the vast accident data of Sweden's Folksam insurance company. With over 700,000 recorded accident data, including 34,000 deaths. Folksam had classified some cars as potentially subjecting their occupants to a severe risk and degree of injury. Folksam recommended that these cars were too dangerous to use. On the blacklist was the VW Beetle 1200-1500, although the later design Super Bug type cars were rated safer. The earlier Beetle inspired Ford Pinto and many small car rivals to join a burgeoning market sector. The Beetle was very popular in America. Why didn't Nader and Dowie warn the 1977 public that the VW Beetle had a poor accident safety record also? Why wasn't Beetle being recalled? Mainly because people knew it was a small car, and accepted the risks.

Road & Track's April 1972 evaluation provided some common sense. In a collision between a motorcycle and Beetle, the Bug wouldn't get squashed, but it probably would against a Buick. The Buick wouldn't like being tapped by a truck, which in turn couldn't cope with a freight train! Small cars are small cars – to single out a particular model and use selected evidence to claim that car is dangerous is quite an assertion. However, the safety lobby was calling for the Pinto's blood, they wanted a recall now! The NHTSA wasn't biting, the body had looked at the accident data. It considered Pinto's accident rate as normal, with no basis to force a recall. However, the crowds weren't satisfied and shouted even louder for a recall. As the chief government safety body, the NHTSA felt it had to do something, or at least be seen to be doing something. That something was the Bullet Test.

The NHTSA got hold of a full-size 1971 Chevy Impala, loaded the front end with weights so the nose went low, and turned on the headlamps hoping for a spark. They ran this car into a '72 Pinto with full gas tank at 35mph. Not the original 20mph, or proposed 30mph, but 35mph! The authority wanted to simulate a worst case scenario with a fire. This they achieved, the Pinto exploded into flames. There was enough to trigger a mandatory recall. The NHTSA had succumbed to lobby group and public pressure. Its hands were clean, the crash test had spoken.

The Bullet Test flew against normal NHTSA procedure, and was in no way an official test standard. No small car at the time would have passed. Proving their unorthodox manner, directed at failing Pinto, at around the same time in 1978, the NHTSA carried out a rear end fuel system integrity test on the BMW 320i subcompact. A new design with the saddlebag tank. However, in this case they used the normal moving barrier test at 30mph, not with an actual bullet car. They also only part-filled the BMW's tank with non-flammable Stoddard liquid, not real gasoline as with the Pinto.

The Bullet Test was overseen by NHTSA engineer Lee Strickland. In 1996 Strickland was questioned why the NHTSA subjected Pinto to such a hard test. His reply was that you shouldn't get off for shoplifting, just because your friends did. All other small car automakers were happy with the NHTSA's conduct, because they knew by focusing solely on Ford and the Pinto, the inadequacies of their cars would be overlooked. The NHTSA gave the public a false sense of security that the small car they were driving was safe, as long as it wasn't a Pinto, because according to the NHTSA and Mark Dowie, the Pinto was the only unsafe car sold in North America. As things stood, Ford did a voluntary recall in June 1978 of 1.5 million Pintos and Mercury Bobcats. The similarly engineered Mustang II and longer Pinto wagon weren't recalled.

Under the recall FoMoCo added a plastic gas tank shield made of polyethylene, a longer filler tube and an improved tank filler seal. Would these changes have helped Mrs Gray and Richard Grimshaw? Probably not, but at least the Center for Auto Safety's conscience was clear. If the objective was to raise the passive safety of small cars, econoboxes like the VW Rabbit and Ford Escort were probably not even as safe as the Pinto, Vega and Gremlin. The reason was fuel economy.

Come 1979/80 and the World went through another OPEC-instigated fuel crisis. Gas mileage became paramount, as all talk turned to CAFE and EPA city/highway numbers. Reducing vehicle weight became key. In such inflationary and recessionary times, people were willing to shoehorn themselves into the smallest, cheapest car they could. Heavens, they even started to covet Rabbit diesels!

Calspan did an offset crash test between a subcompact Rabbit and a compact AMC Concord. The VW's structure deformed heavily, putting front seat occupants at major risk. Front 35mph impact tests of the Renault Le Car by the NHTSA, showed HIC (Head Injury Criteria) in excess of 1000. This would suggest a very real chance of a fatality. The same government body tested the Renault Fuego. The Fuego displayed severe safety cell deformation, and HIC readings much worse than even the Le Car.

The worst car for safety that the NHTSA ever tested, on record by a government authority, is the Peugeot 504. Subjected to the standard 35mph front impact crash test, the body structure deformed to such a degree that the structure had to be cut to extract the crash test dummies. Even though all these imported cars behaved very poorly in crash testing, there was not one safety recall concerning the inadequacy of their safety cell structures. Ralph Nader and the Center for Auto Safety were silent. After all, they were imported cars. Ironically, pre-downsized rear drive domestics, like the AMC Concord and Chrysler F-body (Aspen & Volare), displayed relatively strong survival cells. There is no question that passive safety was compromised, with the weight-saving, lighter econocars of the '80s.

The Ford Pinto was unlucky in that its peak popularity, coincided with a time when there were still many old school fullsize 4000lb plus domestic cars on the road. The use of the law, and nature of case law was also unfair. In State of Indiana v Ford Motor Co (1978), a driver had left his gas filler cap on the roof. He stopped the '73 Pinto to retrieve the fallen cap, when a Chevy van struck the Pinto, killing three teenage girls. The family received a recall notice after the accident. Realistically, it seems unlikely the Ford fixes fitted in the Pinto's recall would have helped in this case. Showing the madness of Mark Dowie, no magic $11 part can make a 2000lb car withstand the impact of a 5000lb van.

Further madness was displayed by the State of Indiana attacking Ford, in the criminal court for a product liability case. A former NHTSA boss testified on Ford's behalf, stating the Pinto was as safe as other small cars of the day. In 1980, Ford was found not guilty of murder. There has not been another product liability case brought against a corporation in criminal court in the years since. The sensational, melodramatic act of accusing a company of murder was legally ill advised, and represented a misuse of the criminal court system. A further case of legal madness was the 1984 example of unrealistic expectations concerning small car safety. The facts involved a young woman who was driving her 1975 Pinto. An auto accident left her permanently brain damaged. She received her injury in a frontal crash, where as a driver she was sharing the two seat front compartment with two girlfriends. That is, three young women were sitting at the front, even though there were only two seats. Not one of the three women was wearing a seatbelt. Even so, Ford were being sued for the Pinto not having, or providing, an airbag. An unusual claim, in the light of the circumstances. No small car of the Pinto's era, import or domestic, had an airbag option.

In light of the jury being sympathetic to the young brain damaged woman, and overlooking the facts, Ford decided to settle out of court for $1.8 million.

As observed by *Road & Track*'s Ron Wakefield, "A strange land, this. We seem to accept anything but the concept of personal responsibility here."[11] Ex Ford public relations man Paul Weaver said Ford should have taken a more assertive stance, and defended itself in public. The statement should have been made, that Pinto had a similar gas tank design and placement as other small car rivals. In addition, it should also have been stated that Pinto was equally safe as small car rivals. It had a similar incidence of fire-related deaths as Vega and Gremlin. It became common in later years for companies to take this assertive approach. For example, to answer the *Supersize Me* documentary, McDonalds' boss made a TV commercial stating that the family restaurant offered a range of healthy choices. Plus, if one ate supersize serves, three times a day, several days a month, then obviously one would become unwell.

Sadly, objectivity and common sense were greatly absent during the Pinto fiasco. And naturally, there would be little reason shown in trial by Tinseltown. Hollywood offered two movies on the Pinto subject, which merely maintained the status quo Pinto exploding gas tank myth. There was the 1984 comedy spoof *Top Secret!,* starring Val Kilmer. It included a scene where a military vehicle slightly tapped the rear bumper of a red Pinto. As expected, the Pinto immediately exploded in flames.

Top Secret! made a special effort to display the rear deck Pinto nameplate badge. Just so you knew it wasn't a Vega or Gremlin. The second film was the 1991 courtroom drama *Class Action*, starring Gene Hackman. A high-minded drama that lifted its plot essence directly from Mark Dowie's 'Pinto Madness' *Mother Jones* article. The plot concerned legal action against an automaker that produced allegedly defective station wagons. The allegation was that such wagons exploded when struck, while making a left turn.

An eccentric foreign designer was put on the witness stand, and mentioned how the company was aware that there was a fault with the station wagon's electrical system, whereby being struck while indicating a left turn was like pressing a detonator. The manufacturer used cost-benefit analysis to decide it was cheaper to fight court cases than to redesign the car and rejoin the human race. Surprisingly, Mark Dowie didn't write the screenplay.

It has been asked why the Pinto exploding gas tank myth has been allowed to stand for so very long. Especially since the myth has no facts to support it, beyond a biased and hysterical media. Perhaps the answer should be left to Hollywood. As was said in the movie *The Man Who Shot Liberty Valance*, 'When the legend becomes fact, print the legend.'

Ford items of interest

Gapp Online
www.gapponline.net
A website started by son Jeff Gapp, that shares and seeks information and pictures concerning Wayne Gapp's racing career. It was a career which involved the Gapp & Roush partnership, plus well-known Ford Maverick (Tijuana Taxi), Mustang II and Pinto Pro Stock drag race cars.

Roush Automotive Collection
www.roushcollection.com
Preserving the historical timeline of the achievements of Cactus Jack Roush. Includes the Pro Stock days of Gapp & Roush, and NASCAR exploits through the years.

The Mustang II Organization
www.mustangii.org
Established 1997, this online group shows owner cars, Mustang II activities, information, member mailing list and forum links. Join the Mustang II online revolution!

Stang Net
www.stangnet.com
Whatever the year or model, if you like Mustangs this forum is for you. With specific areas for all Mustang generations, including Mustang II.

The Forgotten Pony – Tony's Corral
www.forgottenpony.com
Celebrating Ford's forgotten pony, and showcasing the Mustang II related work of Tony Hall.

Pinto Car Club of America
www.fordpinto.com
With a Ford Pinto & Mercury Bobcat register, online store, classifieds and forums, this is HQ for Pinto and Bobcat devotees.

The Pinto Stampede
www.pintostampede.com
www.facebook.com/PintoStampede
Run by Norm Bagi, this club is for Ford Pinto and Mercury Bobcat owners to get together and celebrate their rides!
Email: bosspinto@pintostampede.com
Cell: 646-408-7526

MotorWeek – Channel PBS
www.motorweek.org
MotorWeek and host John Davis have had many Mustangs, and other Fords, on the PBS show since 1981. A great TV destination for FoMoCo fans.

One could build a Pangra-based Pinto cumulatively, or order a complete Pangra from Huntington Ford. (Courtesy Huntington Ford)

PINTO FRONT CONVERSION KIT
Add custom 'European' elegance in just 4 hours!
REQUIRES ONLY A WRENCH & SCREWDRIVER

Pinto owners can now inexpensively convert their cars' conventional appearance to the extremely distinctive, exclusive **PANGRA** styling. Of particular distinction are the retractable headlights incorporated in the fenders.

Existing Pinto grille, headlamps and bumper fit perfectly into the **PANGRA** custom fiberglass units.

Huntington Ford also offers **PANGRA** Suspension and water-injection Turbocharger Kits.

ONLY
$595
F.O.B. ARCADIA, CA.

KIT INCLUDES:
HOOD ● COWL - WITH AIR SCOOPS ● FENDERS
RETRACTABLE HEADLIGHT MECHANISMS

PINTO PANGRA©

only
by
HUNTINGTON FORD

HUNTINGTON FORD ● 55 W. Huntington Dr. ● Arcadia, Calif. 91006

Please send more information on the Pinto **PANGRA** Kits

NAME_____
ADDRESS_____
CITY_____ STATE/ZIP_____

Pangra – what Pinto is this?!

Running alongside the interest in muscle cars and pony cars during the mid to late '60s, was a greater appreciation for exotic European sportscars. Such machines were often Italian, increasingly mid-engined, and went beyond ye olde upright British MG, Triumph and Austin-Healey. Trouble was, such exotics were expensive. American-engined cars like the Apollo GT, De Tomaso Mangusta and Pantera were cheaper, but still way beyond a Vette. If only a sleek, low hood lined sportster with high output engine and real handling could be available for upscale pony car money? Such a vehicle was called Pangra, and like big brother Pantera, one could obtain it from a FoMoCo family dealer, but just one … Huntington Ford of Arcadia, California.

In January 1973, *Motor Trend*'s Steve Smith speculated on the nature of this mystery car: "… that other car isn't the '74 Mustang, what is it?[12] The Pangra was a specially developed, low volume production ultra sports subcompact,

based on the humble Pinto. As Steve Smith observed, was not the first Porsche 356 simply a VW Beetle with aspirations? From the get go, Pangra was more advanced than that first draft Porsche. The Pangra was the idea of Huntington Ford general sales manager Jack Stratton. With the muscle car on the slide, and insurance premiums plus pollution controls attacking car lovers, something had to be done. The answer was Pangra.

The Pangra's substance was discernible from the kits that comprised it. Kit #1 cost $495 and brought a Pantera-like front fascia, with flat nose and pop-up headlamps. The standard Pinto grille and bumper were retained. With the Pinto's already Euroesque hatch profile styling, Kit #1 reinforced Pangra's import flavor. Kit #2 afforded a sportier interior, to the tune of $782. There were dash and console amendments, plus Stewart-Warner gages. No superfluous wood trimmings, but a business-like ambiance with digital tach.

Brad Fagan owns two of the remaining five Pangras. The black car rides on American Racing Torque Thrust rims, wrapped in B F Goodrich Traction TA radials. Billet center caps add decoration. (Courtesy Brad Fagan)

Top: The braking system of this Pangra has been upgraded to Granada 5 bolt front disks with GM metric calipers. Mustang 10in drums now live out back. (Courtesy Brad Fagan)

Bottom: The 2-liter Pinto 4 banger has been improved with modern touches to 250bhp net. A Crower cam, 8.5:1 forged pistons and intercooler weren't on the original Pangra. (Courtesy Brad Fagan)

Imports were expected to handle, in keeping with this the $1156 Kit #3 gave Pangra enough self control to put Corvette on the trailer. The Spearco Can Am suspension kit came courtesy of George Spears' Spearco Performance Products. Spearco did a special Mustang II a little later that bore its name. With Pangra, the Pinto's suspension was made over with four adjustable Konis and two Spearco solid swaybars, 0.957in and 0.628in front and rear respectively. Pangra sat 2in lower than stock, and rolling stock equaled 13 x 5.5in cast machined, gold anodized slot mags, wearing Austrian 185/70HR-13in Semperit radials.

These kits were cumulative, with each successive number adding to the previous kit's contents. Kit #4 cost $1896 and included a turbo conversion for the 2-liter Pinto mill, by land speed record racer A K Miller. Miller's wisdom brought a custom cast iron intake manifold, downpipe and Garrett turbo. It was a

suck-through turbo arrangement, with fuel supplied by a solitary two-barrel Weber 5200 carb. Boost was limited to 10psi, and detonation was kept at bay by water injection.

The cam of choice was an Erson 290AS solid lifter job, with 0.532in lift on intake and exhaust sides, plus 217 degrees duration at 0.050in lift. With a 7:1 CR, the 2-liter made 175 net horses at 5500rpm (285bhp gross according to Huntington Ford), and 220lb/ft (net) at 3600rpm. The turbo kit and Spearco suspension parts were the only things Huntington Ford didn't build or engineer in-house.

As many as 200 Pangra-related kits, Kit #1 being the most popular, were sold from Huntington Ford across the

The Pangra's 2.0 I4 now has a custom intake manifold for a Holley 650CFM double pumper. A MSD coil, Mallory Unilite distributor and HyFire VI ignition with boost retard keep the engine safe. (Courtesy Brad Fagan)

AK Miller was experimenting with the high octane performance qualities of propane gas. Hence the Pangra's fuel use windshield exemption sticker. A handy quality in low lead, and soon no lead, low octane gasoline America. (Courtesy Brad Fagan)

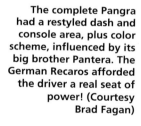

The complete Pangra had a restyled dash and console area, plus color scheme, influenced by its big brother Pantera. The German Recaros afforded the driver a real seat of power! (Courtesy Brad Fagan)

country. However, one could only get a complete Pangra from Huntington Ford. For around $4600, a buyer received a car with kits #1 through #4 included, plus West German made Recaros, custom made console and dash. Only around 35 of these ultra Pangras were made, and just five survive today.

The Pangra wasn't cheap, it cost $400 more than a base 400ci Trans Am. However, it wasn't expensive, being a grand less than the much slower accelerating, 'not so uber after all' Porsche 914S. Porsche, no substitute? Yes, there was! Huntington Ford only offered the Pangra in 1973 and 1974. The Pangra became yet another victim of the 1973-74 fuel crisis, inflation and ensuing recession that killed off so many factory and dealer performance specials in 1974. AMX, Z-28, SD 455 and poor Pangra.

There was no sadness in driving a Pangra. It was a whole car greater than the sum of its parts. *Motor Trend* found it rode and handled very well, and at 7.5

seconds for 0-60 mph, it held a three second advantage over the Porsche 914S. The journal also disclosed an impressive 15.4 second ¼ mile at 92mph, with 125mph top speed to follow. All this with 18mpg fuel economy, or twice that of a V8 gas guzzler. Pangra was also ready to meet 1975's draconian federal pollution standards. No wonder everyone was looking to turbocharging for the future.[13]

It seemed little Huntington Ford achieved an emissions, performance and economy panacea, far superior to the 2.3 Lima turbo in the 1979 Foxstang. Downsides with Pangra included turbo lag. It wasn't quite as bad as the lag with a Porsche 930. Then again, the Pangra's brakes weren't quite as good as the four-wheel 11in plus disks of the Porsche 914S. Pangra used Pinto/Mustang II's 9.3in front disk/9.0in rear drum combo, one of Pangra's few compromises.

The familiar four-speed Hummer gearbox was yet another Pangra item of

Above: A four-speed only car, the Pangra had full Stewart-Warner instrumentation that included a futuristic LED tach. (Courtesy Brad Fagan)

Left: In its exotic European role, the Pangra was more successful than the mid '80s SVO Foxstang. Huntington Ford made it special. (Courtesy Brad Fagan)

Germanic origin, and was no hardship. Combined with the pre MPG 3.55 rear end, performance was never less than spirited. Pangra was only one second slower to sixty than the 1973 Pantera, or the 1976 North American Porsche 930. How's that for Ford Total Performance?! The driver's left hand worked a handlebar to raise or lower the pop up headlamps. The right hand worked a real handbrake. A true exotic indeed.

Pangra's flat nose boosted length to 174.5in, but height was a limbo low 47.7in. Width remained a stock Pinto 69.4in, wide enough for a mid-engined aura. *Motor Trend*'s 0.78g skidpad reading was enough to embarrass a mid engine Euro exotic of the day. After all, Pangra's front and rear tracks measured 57in. The 2300lb bolide, like Pantera, was a Ford where it counted. The sturdy 2-liter Pinto mill could be trusted, so too the '72 Ford 6¼in open differential.

In making a European style performance car, the Pangra had a head start by being based on the Ford Pinto. FoMoCo was a domestic pioneer when it came to design using the metric system. The Ford Model A was built in 100ths of an inch, or a decimal inch. The earlier Model T was designed in 64ths of an inch. Ford was the earliest of the Big Four to formally go metric, starting in the late '60s. Ford's Pinto, as a car and engine, was a metric pioneer. The Chevy Chevette was only partly so.[14]

Pangra also had pedigree. The early '72 based Pinto Pangra proto car driven by magazines, had a roof wing mounted in the fall of 1973. So fitted, 1973 Indy 500 champ Gordon Johncock tested Pangra's top speed at California's Ontario road circuit. Running true to its exotic nature, Pangra joined the Ferrari Daytona and Pantera in saying arriverderci in 1974. *Road & Track* only achieved a 0-60mph time of 7.2 seconds, and equally mediocre 10.5mpg, out of the Daytona in November that year. Is it a Pinto? Is it a Ford? No Henry, it's a Pangra!

Hidemi Aoki with
Motor Max's Fresh
Cherries Mustang II
and Granada. (Courtesy
www.motormaxtoy.com
& www.nepoeht.com)

Spec tables

1971 Ford Pinto

Base price: $1919	
Option prices: 2.0-liter engine ($50), front disks ($32), A70-13 tires ($87), Luxury Decor Group ($130), AM radio ($61), fold-down rear seat ($36)	
Engine: 122ci (2-liter) inline four, SOHC, cast iron head & block, 2bbl carb, 8.6:1 CR (regular gas), 100bhp @ 5600rpm, 120lb/ft @ 3600rpm	
Gearbox: Four-speed all synchro German Hummer (1st) 3.65 (2nd) 1.97 (3rd) 1.37 (4th) 1.00 (rear axle) 3.55:1	
Suspension front: Unequal length control arms, coils, tube shocks	
Suspension rear: Leaf sprung live axle, tube shocks	
Steering: Rack and pinion (manual) 4.2 turns lock to lock	
Dimensions: Length 163in / width 69.4in / height 50.1in / wheelbase 94in	
Weight: 2170lb	
Weight distribution: 55.5/44.5%	
Brakes: 9.3in disk (front), 9.0 x 1.4in drum (rear) – non boosted	
Wheels & tires: 13x5in steel 4 bolt rims / Goodyear A70-13	
Performance: 0-60mph 10.5 seconds ¼ mile 17.6 seconds at 76mph Top speed 99mph	
Economy: 24mpg overall (regular gas)	
Source: *Car and Driver* November 1971	

Known internally as 'Lee's Car' (Lee Iacocca), the Pinto was Ford's subcompact American designed and built answer to VW Beetle et al. It courted controversy, but provided safe and economical small car ownership to millions. Can a commercially successful small car be made in America? Yes, it can!

1976 Ford Mustang II Cobra II

Base price: 1976 Mustang II V8 $3992	
Option prices: Cobra II pack ($312), automatic ($239), power steering ($117), power brakes ($54), alloy wheels ($96), leatherette steering wheel ($33), AM radio / eight track tape deck ($192)	
Engine: 302ci V8, OHV, cast iron head & block, 2bbl carb, 8.0:1 CR (unleaded gas), 134bhp @ 3600rpm, 247lb/ft @ 1800rpm	
Gearbox: C4 3 speed automatic (1st) 2.46 (2nd) 1.46 (3rd) 1.00 (rear axle) 3.00:1	
Suspension front: Unequal length control arms, coils, tube shocks, 0.815in swaybar	
Suspension rear: Leaf sprung live axle, tube shocks, 0.75 in swaybar	
Steering: Rack and pinion (powered) 3.3 turns lock to lock	
Dimensions: Length 175in / Width 70.2in / Height 49.7in / Wheelbase 96.2in	
Weight: 3460lb	
Weight Distribution: 56.1/43.9%	
Brakes: 9.3in vent disk (front), 9.0 x 2in drum (rear) – boosted and using HD Pinto wagon rear drums	
Wheels & tires: 13 x 5.5in forged alloy 4 bolt rims / Firestone Steel Radial 500 195/70R-13	
Performance: 0-60mph 9.9 seconds ¼ mile 17.71 seconds at 78.26mph Top Speed 101mph	
Economy: 18.1mpg overall (RT cycle using unleaded gas)	
Source: *Road Test* March 1976	

To spice up the Mustang II for 1976, the Cobra II package evoked nostalgia for the 1965 Shelby Mustang GT 350. Cobra II was developed by BORT Inc. It was added to cars by Jim Wanger's Motortown Corp during 1976.

Endnotes

(Indicated by superscript numbers in the main text)

(1)   Roger Huntington, 'Detroit Notebook,' *Autocar* 1974 August 31 p44
(2)   Bob McClurg, 'Dyno Don Unveils The First Mustang II PRO/STOCK,' *Drag Racing* USA 1974 June p45
(3)   'Ford and Pontiac Bring Back The Racer Look,' *Autoweek* 1978 January 13 p5
(4)   Robert Schilling, 'Detroit's Economy Car Gap (Part 2),' *Motor Trend* 1967 April p80
(5)   'Ford and Chevy level their sights on Volkswagen,' *Car and Driver* 1970 September p28
(6)   '15,000 Mile Comparison Test: Chevrolet Vega Versus Ford Pinto,' *Car and Driver* 1971 November p24
(7)   'The Little Cars,' *Consumer Reports* 1971 January p8
(8)   'R&T Specifications 1975,' *Road & Track* 1975 February p92
(9)   Drew Hardin, Sema Pioneers Bill Neumann, December 2003 p53
(10)   'The Ultimate street car??? JAWS,' *Super Stock and Drag Illustrated* 1975 October p31
(11)   Ron Wakefield, 'Another bizarre auto-accident lawsuit,' *Motor* 1984 w/e May 19 p25
(12)   Steve Smith, 'The Pinto, The Porsche, And The Pangra,' *Motor Trend* 1973 January p37
(13)   Ibid.
(14)   Kenneth F. Weaver, 'How Soon Will We Measure In Metric?' National Geographic 1977 August p293

A 2016 Mustang Roush Stage 3. The little Deuce helped the Mustang nameplate survive into the 21st century. (Courtesy John Zofko https://www.youtube.com/watch?v=_UFDt05fvg0)

Also from Veloce Publishing –

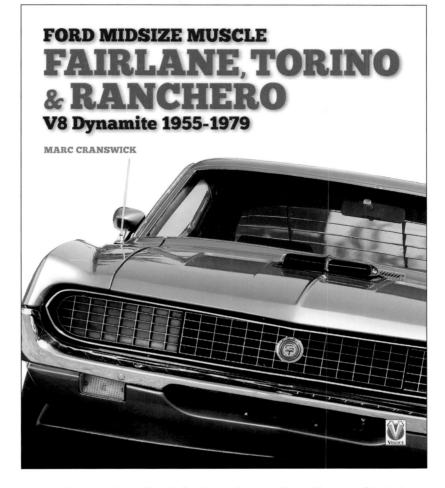

The evolution of Ford's family car through the golden era of Detroit.
The book tells how Henry took the no-frills Fairlane, added more zing to
create the Torino, and satisfied America's luxury desires with the LTD II; and
follows the evolution of Ford's midsize muscle cars, to the creation of the
first car-based pickup – the Ranchero.

ISBN: 978-1-845849-29-0
Hardback • 25x20.7cm • 176 pages • 229 pictures

For more information and price details, visit our website at www.veloce.co.uk
• email: info@veloce.co.uk • Tel: +44(0)1305 260068

Also from Veloce Publishing –

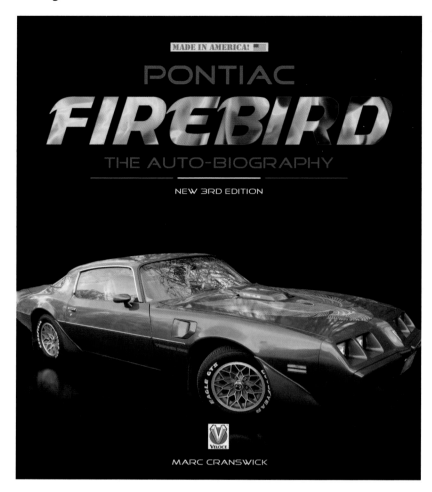

An updated and enlarged examination of the complete model history
of General Motor's upmarket F body variant. Close attention is paid to both
regular and high level model variants (Formula & Trans Am), and how Pontiac
made its Firebird unique. Includes 81 new images.

ISBN: 978-1-78711-003-8
Hardback • 25x20.7cm • 208 pages • 335 pictures

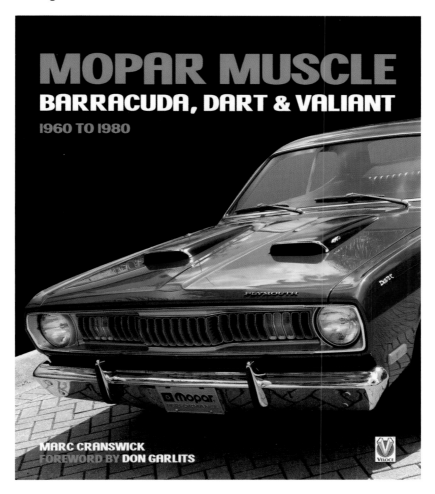
For more information and price details, visit our website at www.veloce.co.uk
• email: info@veloce.co.uk • Tel: +44(0)1305 260068

125

Also from Veloce Publishing –

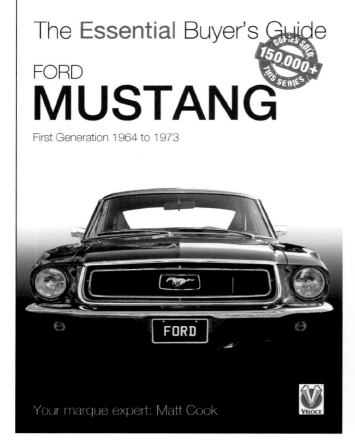

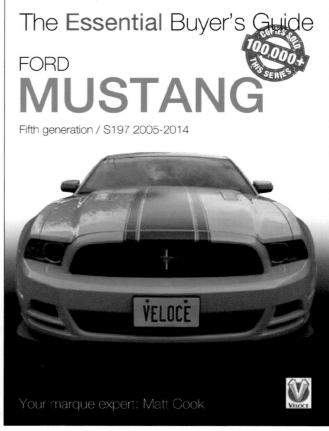

ISBN: 978-1-845844-47-9
Paperback • 19.5x13.9cm • 64 pages • 106 colour pictures

ISBN: 978-1-845847-98-2
Paperback • 19.5x13.9cm • 64 pages • 108 colour pictures

Having these books in your pocket is just like having a real marque expert by your side. Benefit from the author's years of Mustang ownership, learn how to spot a bad car quickly, and how to assess a promising car like a professional. Get the right car at the right price!

Index